how to craft
successful
business
presentations
and effective **public speaking**

Dedication

With thanks to those colleagues who helped me get to my feet the first time and showed me how, and to those who have listened to me in such circumstances since.

how to craft
successful
business
presentations
and effective **public speaking**

patrick forsyth

foulsham
LONDON • NEW YORK • TORONTO • SYDNEY

foulsham

The Publishing House, Bennetts Close, Cippenham,
Slough, Berkshire, SL1 5AP, England

Foulsham books can be found in all good bookshops and direct
from www.foulsham.com

ISBN 13: 978-0-572-03218-0
ISBN 10: 0-572-03218-8

Copyright © 2006 Patrick Forsyth

Cover photograph © Superstock

A CIP record for this book is available from the British Library

Printed in Great Britain by CPD (Wales) Ltd, Ebbw Vale.

Talking and eloquence are not the same:

to speak, and to speak well are two things.

Ben Johnson

Acknowledgements

Knowledge advances by steps, not by leaps.
Lord Macaulay

No speeches, but always, when writing this sort of material, I finish with the distinct feeling that I would not have been able to complete the brief, and indeed did not do so, alone.

I am in a position to comment on such matters only because of the help I have received from others along the way. In this case numbers of people who prompted me towards public speaking in the past, and many others who I have learned from over the years. Thanks are also due to the many people I have met in the course of my consulting and training work – many conversations and questions with participants on both public and in-company seminars and courses on the topic of presentation skills have added to my knowledge and experience of how things work in this area. Thank you all.

Finally, writing – and the process that goes with it of getting published – is for the most part a solitary process. Collaboration with other writers can be both useful and enjoyable. In this context I would like to thank Frances Kay, always an admirable collaborator, and who assisted in getting this particular work off the ground.

Patrick Forsyth
Touchstone Training & Consulting
28 Saltcote Maltings
Maldon
Essex CM9 4QP
United Kingdom

About the author

Given the topic of this book it is perhaps appropriate to mention the author's credentials in offering advice in this area. Patrick Forsyth runs Touchstone Training & Consultancy, an independent firm specialising in the improvement of business performance, and focusing primarily on marketing, sales, communications and management skills.

As a consultant and trainer of more than 25 years' experience, Patrick has fronted a great variety of events and as a trainer he has led countless management training courses, not least on the topic of presentation skills. Many of these have been for individual companies and others in the form of public seminars for organisations such as The Institute of Management (and similar bodies overseas, for example The Singapore Institute of Management). He has also spoken at many conferences, some public events, some for specialist bodies such as Central Law Training and others for individual organisations. Training has involved him addressing audiences ranging from a dozen people from one company to several hundred from many different organisations. One major event involved an audience of more than two thousand plus video links to more people in two other cities, with everything (or the gist of it!) being translated simultaneously into Spanish.

His training work has always included many workshops designed to develop participants' skills in making effective presentations. In addition, among a number of successful books he has written, two other books are on this topic, *The Management Speaker's Handbook* (How to Books), which provides a template for typical corporate speechmaking occasions, and *Hook Your Audience* (Management Pocketbooks) – the latter looking at the use of humorous anecdotes and examples to enhance or enliven business presentations.

Like most presenters he has found that things have not always gone well. He has on occasion been the only person to make it to an event (because of heavy snow); opened his file at the start of a presentation to find material prepared for a different event in front of him; spoken by candlelight in a power cut and paused for various venue catastrophes ranging from fire alarms (real and imaginary) to falling ceilings. Despite such occurrences he continues to make presentations, and tries hard to remember the advice of David Martin: *The golden rule for all presenters is to imagine that you are in the audience.*

Contents

Introduction

> *The human brain is a wonderful thing. It starts working the moment you are born and never stops until you stand up to speak in public.*
>
> Sir **George Jessel**

We all have to do lots of things we do not like. Some are just distasteful things like unblocking the sink or cleaning someone else's ring off the bath, others are worse – things we feel seriously ill equipped to do well.

Take speaking: we can all have a chat, swap gossip or say, *'What time do you call this?'* to the postman, but sometimes we may have to do something rather more formal. But ask many people to stand up and address an audience and they go to pieces, or to Reykjavik – anything at all rather than do it.

It can be done however. Anyone can make an acceptable, workmanlike speech and many find that it is something at which they can excel if they go about it the right way. How to do that is the subject of this book. Few people are natural public speakers; and those that make it look easy tend to do so because they work at it.

But stand up totally unprepared and, oh dear, things can go wrong. People stumble, they hesitate, and they sweat. They begin every other sentence with the superfluous word *'Basically'.* Asked to comment on some project, they say *'Um, er ... at this moment in time we are making considerable progress with the necessary preliminary work prior to the establishment of the initial first phase of work'* when they mean *'We aim to start soon'.*

Just when they should be impressing their audience with their expertise and confidence, and making them interested in what they have to say, they upset or confuse them. Exactly what is said and how it is put matters, indeed there may be a great deal hanging on it. As Bob Hope used to say of his early performances, *'If the audience liked you, they didn't applaud, they let you live'*.

At worst, people go on too long, their explanation explains nothing and where they are going is wholly unclear. Some fidget endlessly, others remain stock still gripping the table or lectern in front of them until their knuckles go white and fear rises from them like a mist. Still others are apt to pick holes in people in the audience, or their noses. If they use slides, then they can only be read from the back of the room with a telescope, a fact made worse by their asking brightly *'Can you see all right at the back?'* despite the fact that there is precious little they can do about it if the answer is *'no'*, and in any case they should not be asking, they should know their slides are legible. They barely pause for breath, as they rush from one word to the next, many of them inappropriately chosen and as many more too long. Indeed, the only long word of which some speakers appear ignorant is rehearsal.

Of course, a lucky few believe that making a speech or presentation is second nature. They know they can wing it. They are convinced that they know their stuff and how to put it over. The first rule then for the inappropriately overconfident is, of course, to assume that the audience is as thick as they look and will, provided the right level of impenetrable gobbledegook is hit, instantly conclude that they are in the presence of a master.

Winging it means that if they want people to actually understand even the gist of what is said, then some care must be taken. So, they talk v-e-r-y s-l-o-w-l-y; use simple words, and generally proceed on the basis that the audience have the brains of a retarded dormouse. They spell out complicated bits in CAPITAL LETTERS, speaking MORE LOUDLY as they do so. Though they are always careful not to be condescending, as that will upset people (you *do know* what condescending *means*, don't you?).

For this kind of speaker, being on their feet is something to savour. They need only the briefest of introductions and they are away, moving quickly past the first slide without noticing that it is upside down, the coins in their trouser pocket rattling at 90 decibels and the audience hanging on their every repetitive mannerism as they mutter to themselves *'If he scratches his backside whilst stood on one leg again, I'm walking out'*. It makes lesser mortals feel all too sadly inadequate – even the famous: it was Mark Twain who reportedly said, *'It normally takes me three weeks to prepare a good impromptu speech'*. Poor man. Just as well he was a good writer.

But even speakers convinced of their own abilities, however wrongly they hold that view, should not hog all the opportunities for themselves just because they are fun. They should give others a chance. Next time someone says *'Will you give the toast?'*, they may hand over the task to whoever displays the least enthusiasm (maybe to you?). It will do them good they think; and they may feel that there is nothing like inflicting sheer terror on a friend or colleague to make them feel superior.

Putting someone in front of an important audience knowing that they would rather chew off their own fingers than sit and listen to someone who cannot make the simplest point clear, is rather like pushing them into a lion's den. Without an understanding of how to go about it in the right way, they will be in deep, deep trouble. No audience will warm to a speaker who is ill prepared and who flounders through a speech that is tedious, confusing and poorly delivered. And nor will they if the speaker is poor through unthinkingly believing they can wing it. Furthermore, no poor speaker is likely to magically acquire the requisite skills instantaneously in the few seconds between being introduced and rising to their feet to speak.

So, if you are not in fact a natural, and few people are, you need to give it some thought before you get to your feet; once you are actually in the lion's den it is a little late to discover that salvation is not guaranteed by saying *'Nice pussycat'*.

The way forward

Now, all that said, making a good speech or presentation can be exhilarating. Being able to do so is a life skill and can stand you in good stead in many different circumstances from addressing a staff meeting at work, to making a speech at a wedding or at a fundraising charity event. This book is designed to act as an antidote to the problems of public speaking. It will help you speak at work or leisure, whether you are new to the process or seeking to extend your skills. It will help calm nerves and remove the typical fear of such things as drying up, running out of time (or material) and leaving out a key point. It sets out clear, systematic guidance as to how to view the process and how to create and deliver a speech suitable to the occasion in a way that informs and impresses. It provides proven guidance that will enable you to sit down at the end of your next speech or presentation knowing that what you have put over has achieved its purpose and represents a job well done.

An opportunity

When you must speak in public and are able to do so well, you turn something that could be traumatic into something that is a real opportunity. In a business context, presentations have been described as: *The business equivalent of an open goal.* (A character in the excellent Video Arts training film, *I wasn't prepared for that,* says this). It is true; not only of business presentations but of any sort of public speech. It puts the situation memorably too, and is a thought worth holding as you read on.

What follows is not just designed to help you get by, or minimise the difficulties. It is designed to help you maximise the opportunity presented by that open goal, and to make the process of doing so manageable.

So, do read on; you have nothing to lose but your reservations.

CHAPTER 1

On Your Feet

*I am the most spontaneous speaker in the world
because every word, every gesture, and every retort
has been carefully rehearsed.*

George Bernard Shaw

All formal presentations (or speeches, repeating both words all the time will be avoided) involve a group. Matters that you could sit down and run through with one other person, perhaps sitting across the desk or round the kitchen table, are straightforward by comparison. Actually, that is a simplification. Many meetings, and the messages that are communicated in them, are not simple to conduct 'off the top of your head', and some of the issues that this book investigates are applicable in the one-to-one situation as well as for presentations. However, let that pass for the moment. It is the group that makes the difference to many people: a sea of faces, expecting .... what? Are they apprehensive? Hostile? Determined to put one over on us? But we are getting ahead of ourselves. We must be clear initially not only about why presentations are so important, but accept that we can influence their outcome and make them work. In fact, as we will see, their importance goes beyond just getting a message across; though even that may not be inherently straightforward. Furthermore, a presentation will say a good deal more than is involved in just putting over the content of the message, and it will also put out all sorts of subsidiary impressions. It is the audience that influences every aspect of what must be done to make formal speaking effective. In this short chapter a number of premises are addressed which are important background to the detail that follows.

The reasons for presentations

Consider a typical organisation. It can be large or small. It matters little exactly what it does. It could be yours. On a particular day, or during a typical week, some of the items scheduled in the diaries of various executives might include:

- •)) A presentation at a departmental meeting. Perhaps morale is a little low, there are changes to announce, belt-tightening to be instigated or new systems to be explained. The feeling may be that the group will resent or be indifferent to what must be done – yet if the reasons for the message are sound and are put over effectively then the announcement can prompt important changes and lead to improved results.

- •)) A presentation of the annual plan for a section or division is to be made to the Board. Perhaps the hierarchy makes this difficult, perhaps the section feels it is not a major player, perhaps time to make the case and explain the details is limited – *what will they say about the budget?* Despite such feelings the whole of the next operational period will be affected by it and its success, or lack of it. It must go well.

- •)) A presentation is to be made to a major customer. A significant percentage of the annual turnover is dependent on this customer's loyalty, yet the market is increasingly competitive, product and service are being subjected to a harsh appraisal; the customer's judgement will inevitably be affected by the quality of the presentation – a good one will be interpreted as indicative of good service to come, a poor one might put the whole relationship in question, and there are eager competitors waiting on the sidelines.

- •)) A short briefing session is scheduled to explain details of the organisation's move to new offices. The move is being made for all the right reasons, yet inevitably poses short-term problems of organising for, and coping with, the move itself. It also raises personal fears in some people as to what the new place will be like and where individuals will sit. If people co-operate enthusiastically the whole move will go more smoothly – they need to accept the move and see the advantages.

These four are typical of the sort of thing that takes place in organisations everywhere day in, day out. Such a list might include a dozen more situations: a press briefing, a training session, meetings to give advance notice of changes, to canvass support or issue instructions. It could also include significant public relations opportunities such as someone being invited to speak at a conference. Social matters may be involved: a retirement party or a welcome to a new employee, all demanding that an appropriate presentation is made.

So it is too with non-business events. You may belong to an association, chair a committee, have a daughter about to be married or a dozen other things all of which involve you rising to your feet and trying to inform and impress. All such situations involve getting things right and can have a lot hanging on them. At a wedding, for example, the best man who takes his role seriously and who does his preparation will be able to enjoy watching the wedding video again and again. If he neglects thinking his speech through and attempts to wing it, then he risks forever reaching for the fast forward button whenever the video is played.

In all these cases the importance of what is said and how it comes over – its quality – is very clear. And, even in a business context, it going well is not simply of corporate importance, it is also of personal import for whoever is on their feet. Reputations will be enhanced or diluted in the process, the effect is on the outward aspect of corporate profile – and because of this, speaking skill is what one might call a career skill: that is, something that may affect your ability to shine in your current job, and your ability to influence moving beyond it. But there are also more personal implications. For the inexperienced, uninformed or untried speaker the process is inclined to be not just difficult. It can also be literally frightening; and the fact that some of the common fears are – if analysed – irrational may well help to dispel them not one jot. We know, if we think about it for a moment, that the ground is *not* actually going to open up under our feet so that we sink without trace – though there may be moments when we pray that it will!

Making it go well

So, two things can be taken as given. The first is that presentations are important. This may seem to be something that it is impossible to ignore (it is not; more of this later) and is certainly amongst the reasons that mean giving presentations can be a traumatic process. If you are in any way wary of them be assured that you are completely normal. Most speakers, even the most experienced, have fears to some degree. With experience comes the ability to deal with those fears, and minimise if not totally remove them.

Secondly, presentations must go well. Let me rephrase that for it must be seen in a specific way: *you* must *make* them go well. Short of delegation – which will never always be possible even for the most senior person – there is no other way.

Furthermore, there may be comparatively few 'born speakers', but there are an increasing number of people who have become able to make a pretty good job of it and many who are more than workmanlike. I am living proof that presentational ability can be acquired, even by the most reluctant person (early in my career it was certainly not something I ever thought I would get involved with, indeed it was something I actively sought to avoid). Those speakers you perhaps regard as naturals almost certainly have one thing in common; they work at it. The many techniques involved (many, as we will see, both straightforward and common sense) really do help. They help both to smooth and polish the presentation itself and to make it psychologically easier to deal with. An understanding of the process, and of the details of what makes it go well, what it is that achieves particular effects, and how to both work at the detail and orchestrate the whole, is the foundation for good performance. Of course, practice helps too, and practice provides more experience more quickly if you understand what is going on, and why what you are doing is working or perhaps currently not quite hitting the mark. The scenarios referred to, and described in the introduction, highlight and contrast the skills needed and the dangers of there being a lack of them.

The first step to improving whatever presentational ability you may currently have is perhaps to see it as something that you *can* change. No-one is born with a ready-made instant appreciation of what makes for good presentation (well, very few people are, and if you were one of those you would be unlikely to be reading this). Like so much else that is worthwhile doing, some effort is required to put yourself in a position to achieve a particular standard or to do better – and this is an ongoing factor with a skill that can really always be improved, there being no such thing as the perfect talk. On the other hand, working at it need not be too onerous or time-consuming and the results you can achieve from a good speech, as has already been indicated, make some effort in this regard very worthwhile. Before moving on to the principles that make the whole process work, two other factors are worth bearing in mind.

Perception *is* reality

Somewhere there is an old saying: *what you see is what you get.* This certainly has relevance here with regard to presentations. Consider by way of example someone selling a service: an accountant, designer or architect perhaps. In such fields it is common for people to have to make competitive presentations – sometimes called beauty parades – as potential clients ascertain which of a short list of potential suppliers they will use.

If such a presentation is inexpertly done, the prospect does not think to themselves, *What an excellent designer, what a shame they cannot make a better presentation.* Rather they say, *What a rotten presentation,*

I bet their design work isn't very good either. In other words, other abilities – and a wide range of them – are judged from people's ability to present. This may not be fair, or even reasonable; but it is without a doubt what happens.

There is no possible response to this but to maximise the impact of presentations carried out to avoid this effect. It does not only occur in overtly sales situations (and in the example it is particularly important because a service by its nature cannot be tested, so the impact of the people involved is crucial), it occurs every time someone gets to their feet to address a group. The audience immediately begins to draw conclusions and make judgements about the person, their general competence and specific abilities. The perceptions that a person engenders are powerfully moulded if they have to present, much more so than in the general business round.

The plus side of this, of course, is that good presentational standards enhance the perception of ability in other areas. By using the appropriate techniques, by putting on a professional show, you can positively and actively build your image generally and increase the chances of acceptance for anything that you may be promoting. This is true externally or internally to the organisation and of any group and circumstance one can think of as an audience. It is a fact that no presenter can afford to forget.

Communication and the audience

Communication, whether one-to-one or with a group, is not easy, or rather the difficulty is to make communication clear and understandable (see what I mean). It is a very easy difficulty to underestimate. Everybody tends to think that they can communicate (rather as you never meet anyone – or certainly no man – who will admit to being a bad driver). After all, we all do it all the time, especially in organisations. But in fact, without care, communication can so easily deteriorate into confusion and misunderstanding. There must be hundreds of examples of communication failure despite the best intentions of the communicator. There are, for example:

- •)) The note left for the milkman saying: *Please deliver an extra pint today. If this note blows away, please ring bell.*

- •)) There is an old story of the journalist, researching a feature on Hollywood, sending a brief telex: 'HOW OLD CARY GRANT?' In due course the message comes back: 'OLD CARY GRANT FINE; HOW ARE YOU?'

- •)) There is also this wonderful phrase, usually attributed to the late ex-US President Nixon: *I know that you understand what you think I said, but I am not sure that you realise that what you heard is not what I meant.*

You can doubtless think of many more. Such stories make a point. Communication is never easy, and on your feet it can be just that bit more difficult as your tongue seems to run away on its own, as nerves overpower precision, and as what started as a careful explanation comes out as garbled and convoluted. Many a speaker has sat down disappointed with the presentation they have just made and *knowing* they could have explained something so much better, one-to-one, or in writing or just with a little longer to get it right. If you have done even a little presenting you do not need to be told that it is different on your feet. You know that this is true.

A good maxim to bear in mind here was said in Roman times by Marcus Fabius Quintilian: *One should not aim at being possible to understand, but at being impossible to misunderstand.*

All this has a bearing on the audience. They want to understand and become restless as well as confused if they do not. The audience is vital to any presenter and we will return to them in later pages; here suffice it to say that there are a number of immediate factors to be borne in mind:

- •))) **Hearing:** this is not perfect; not in the medical sense, but rather because people's concentration wanders. It is just not possible to concentrate continuously (when did your attention last flit away from reading this?), but a speaker who recognises this and intentionally sets out to retain the group's interest will do better than one who ignores the fact

- •))) **Message dilution:** even when people hear, they dilute the message as it is filtered through their existing expectations, knowledge, experience and prejudices; thus new or unfamiliar ideas will need more careful explanation than those that are already well accepted

- •))) **Conclusions:** these may be drawn before the full case has been put across (and the status quo is always difficult to overturn).

That said you can potentially get over these factors. Again much that is to follow here is relevant, but at this stage a few points are worth noting. A presenter must:

- •))) **Look the part:** that means having an appearance which the audience associates with authority, expertise or whatever it is that is trying to be projected, rather than what the speaker regards as comfortable or fashionable. (I would not presume to say much more about how you should look, but would suggest you consider objectively what a powerful part of your own assessment of others this is, and then act appropriately yourself)

- •))) **Come over as a good presenter:** because, as has been said, poor presentation skills have other weaknesses read from them

- •))) **Actually be clear and interesting:** (or any other objective the audience would want you to deploy)

- •))) **Have respect for the audience:** in everything from a seemingly reliable ability to stick to time, to a concentration on what they will find interesting and the most appropriate way to put it across – to any particular group.

The audience, we will find, must be kept perpetually in mind as all the various aspects of presentation are contemplated. Not only that, but a presentation that is genuinely audience oriented will always go down better than something introspective, and may well prove easier to prepare and give as well.

In fact, having harped on about some of the difficulties, there is perhaps one thing worse to contemplate than being on your feet as the Chairperson says, *And now, over to...* feeling hopelessly ill-equipped to undertake the presentation that must follow. And that is to be in the audience when such a presentation is taking place. Really. Think about it; it is not just tedious or boring, it is embarrassing, sometimes in the extreme. Think about what that means: the audience, the group, whoever they are, *want you to succeed*. It is easy to consider the audience as the opposition. However, with a few exceptions perhaps (for example, political situations within an organisation), they are not. They are the reason for the presentation, they want it to go well and you can use this fact to help make it do just that.

This fact is always worth keeping in mind. In the next chapter we turn to the question of the 'nerves' that having to stand up and speak can engender, and not regarding the audience as the opposition is perhaps the first step to overcoming such nerves.

CHAPTER 2

Calming the Nerves

> Overheard: as two speakers spoke together before
> going onto a conference platform:
> *'Are you nervous?'*
> 'No, I don't get nervous, I call it creative
> apprehension.'
> *'Then why have you just come out of the Ladies?'*

As has already been said, speaking in public is often regarded as something traumatic. Indeed it can engender a particularly emotional response in many, and serious (or semi-serious) surveys regularly show it to rank high in terms of overall fears in life, following closely on death and divorce. Few speakers, and this includes the most experienced, would claim to be able to make a presentation with *no* nerves. Some people say a lack of nerves is not only unlikely, it is undesirable; they need some adrenalin to carry them along.

Others have vivid visions of their worst fears:

Imagine: The previous speaker is near to concluding. You cannot seem to concentrate on what he is saying. You run over your opening remarks in your mind for the twenty-seventh time, and, thus distracted, you suddenly hear the Chairman calling your name. You leap to your feet sending your notes scattering to the winds. Panic-stricken, you grovel on the floor and collect them up, half trip up the steps to the platform and take your place behind the lectern. Your rescued pages seem to sit precariously on the edge of the sloping rack, and your hands are shaking so much that you dare not try to straighten them.

You make a start: *Good morning, Gadies and Lentlemen.* Your mouth is dry and you do not seem to be able to catch your breath. You put up your first slide and it is immediately apparent that those in the rear half of the room cannot read it – though everyone notices it is upside down. Having corrected that you are pretty sure they all notice that the word 'agenda' is spelt with a J.

At this point things start to go wrong.

You notice that the clock at the back of the room stopped hours ago and can offer you no guidance, you lose your place in your notes, and turn over to the next page only to find it has got out of order. At which point the papers fall to the floor in what looks like slow motion, and your voice dries completely; the butterflies struggle from your stomach and begin to fly around the room. As one dive-bombs the Chairman, he sounds an air raid siren and …

Wake up. It is not really happening. Indeed hopefully no-one has ever experienced all of this in the same ten minutes. Though mistakes do occur – I remember once driving all the way to Birmingham, a terrible journey in the pouring rain, arriving at the venue I was to speak at only just in time, hastening in and opening my file to check my carefully prepared notes. Carefully prepared they might have been – but they were not for the talk I was scheduled to give that day! Well nobody is perfect.

So, how do you avoid all this?

Making it easier

First, be assured that it is avoidable. All, or certainly the vast majority, of these problems can be avoided. Because, although I have (surely?) exaggerated in the passage above, everyone commonly has some fears and it is appropriate to deal with this aspect of making a presentation now, ahead of getting down to the positive ways in which you can make everything go well. After all, in real life it is difficult to concentrate on a considered approach if you have real reservations about what lies ahead, much less if you are shaking like a leaf. Having said that I am going to cheat and leave one of the cures to a later stage. What is that? In a word: preparation.

It is worth emphasising. Preparation is the surest way to ensure that all goes well and to minimise nerves. The key reason for nerves is the fear that something will go wrong. Prepare well and quite simply you then *know* that a whole range of elements *will* go well. Consider an example from my nightmare above. You will never be put out by discovering that a slide cannot be read from the back of the room, if you have tried it out beforehand. You are less likely to muddle your notes if you number the pages, less likely still if you fasten the pages together or put them securely in some sort of file or binder.

So, we return to the detail of how to undertake your preparation in the next chapter. Before leaving it therefore and dealing with other matters, let me link it to another vital factor: that of confidence. Now confidence is a useful foundation to everything you have to do in speaking formally, and preparation – the security of knowing it is done well, thoroughly and will help – literally breeds confidence. This becomes a virtuous circle. Sound preparation creates confidence, more confidence makes for a better start, a good start boosts your confidence to continue, and … but you get the idea.

It is not just nerves

Regularly in one aspect of my work, that of conducting courses to help people develop their presentation skills, I ask participants what factors they feel make them uneasy about presenting. Be reassured *everyone* has some fears. The commonest stated usually include (in no particular order):

- •)) Butterflies in the stomach

- •)) A dry mouth making it difficult to speak

- •)) Not knowing where to put your hands

•)) Fear of the reaction of the audience

•)) Fear of not having enough material

•)) Fear of not being able to get through the material in the time

•)) Not knowing how loud to pitch your voice

•)) Losing your place

•)) Over- or underrunning on time

•)) Being asked questions you cannot answer

•)) Drying up.

All these main ones that seem to concern people are worth a specific comment (in some cases referring on to more detailed comment to come). Whether such things are real fears for you or just cause minor concern, the view to take of all this is a practical one. There are actions that actually sort out and remove some of these problems, others are helped by the way you organise the speaking environment, something which is explained later in this chapter, and which also has a considerable effect on your ability to overcome any nerves.

What about the fears mentioned above?

•)) **Butterflies in the stomach:** this is a physical manifestation of any worries you may have. In mild form it does no harm and fades as the adrenalin starts to flow when you get underway. On the other hand a number of practical measures undoubtedly help reduce the feeling. Some are seemingly small, perhaps obvious; they do work, however, and may work better when some are used together. They include:

• A few deep breaths just before you start

• No heavy food too soon before you start

• No starvation diets, or the butterflies will be accompanied by rumbles

• No alcohol (some would say very little) before the off.

Plus the confidence of knowing you are well prepared and organised.

•)) **Dry mouth:** again this is a natural reaction, but one simply cured. Just take a sip of water before you start. And never be afraid of asking for, or organising, a supply of water in front of you. Place it where you are least likely to spill it and you may, like me, prefer to avoid the fashionably fizzy waters supplied by many of the venues where speakers often find themselves, especially hotels and conference centres. I am sure it is nice for the audience and offered with good intentions, but it is inclined to make you burp if you are the speaker. The longer the duration of your talk, the more you will need to take the occasional sip. Talking makes you dry and an air-conditioned venue or office compounds the problem. Act accordingly, throughout your talk.

•)) **Somewhere to put your hands:** because somehow they can feel awkward. They seem like disproportionately large lumps at the end of your arms. The trick here is to avoid obvious awkwardness, give yourself something to do with them – hold a pen perhaps – and then forget about them. They should be involved in some gestures, but we will return to that later. Incidentally, it is best that a man should remember that while one hand in a pocket may look all right, both hands in pockets appears slovenly.

Audience reaction: or rather the fear of a negative one. Ask yourself why they should react negatively. The fear may be irrational. It may be because you feel ill prepared – and we have touched on preparation. And anyway remember that audiences hate poor presentations; they *want* you to succeed (see next sub-section to relate matters to the size of the audience).

Not having enough material: this should simply not be a fear. Your preparation will mean you *know* you have not only enough but the right amount of material for the topic and the time.

•))) **Having too much material:** this needs no separate comment from the previous point except that even if you start with too much, preparation should whittle it down to the appropriate amount.

•))) **Not knowing how loud to speak:** this may be a reasonable fear in a strange room, but you can test it – ahead of the meeting find someone to stand at the back and check how you come over until you get the level right. In fact, a moment's thought shows that it is not really a very difficult problem. In other circumstances if a single person came into the room from a door at the far end, you would probably speak to them naturally at just the right level. Try not to worry and think of yourself as addressing the back row (though remember to switch off, I sometimes go home after a day conducting a course and am told, *Don't shout, you are not talking to the back row now*).

•))) **Losing your place:** again there are practical measures to help, apart from knowing your message well, particularly in terms of the exact format of the speaker's notes that you opt to have in front of you (this is of major importance: see Chapter 3).

•))) **Misjudging the timing:** in part an accurate judgement of time comes with practice. If you find it difficult do not despair, you will get better and better at it. Remember timing is important, and particularly not overrunning – a common fault – is a virtue that is, appreciated by many, even in the most entertaining speech; and is vital at, say, a conference when the whole day's events can be put out by one undisciplined speaker. And of course, wear a watch with a clear dial and if necessary synchronise time with the Chairperson.

•))) **Being asked questions you cannot answer:** no-one is expected to be omniscient. Dealing with questions is dealt with in Chapter 7. Here let me make the one point that it is not the end of the world to say: *I don't know* – always an important point for any would-be presenter to accept (though you might have to make some further comment, maybe, *I'll find out and get back to you*).

•)) **Drying up:** here one must address the reason why this might happen. Dry mouth? Pause and have a sip of water, no-one will mind. Indeed always do this if necessary, struggling on risks you ending up choking to a halt and having to pause much longer. Lost your place? If that does not happen you will not dry up. Just nerves? Well, some of the elements now mentioned – and preparation – will help. It is worth remembering here that time often seems to flow at a different rate for presenters and audiences. Often during presentation skills courses, where usually I am using video to record what participants do and prompting discussion about it, people will regularly criticise themselves about one perceived fault: I *dried up at one stage,* they say, *there was an awful great gap.* Yet no-one noticed except them, and often when the video is replayed they cannot even spot where it happened. It just seemed too long to them at the time.

In terms of attitude you should note that you need a practical approach to all these sorts of feelings. Just feeling – *I'm worried* – is difficult to combat. Ask yourself why you are worried and you may well surprise yourself, discovering that there is a practical solution to your fear that will remove or reduce whatever factor is creating the feeling and, at best, allow you to put it right out of your thoughts. With that principle in mind, we turn to another area in which the right action can reduce worries and act to create a comfortable climate in which you can present more easily.

Size of the audience

Initially most people have a clearly graduated reaction to the number of people in the audience. A few are not so bad, you can equate them to a round table meeting, more begins to seem more difficult, and a large number is 'a terrifying sea of faces'. Why so? After all, the job of the speaker is very similar regardless of the numbers present. Not

'lar message to get over, but, to a large extent,
'lar way.

ᴀ large group is to *treat it like a smaller one.*

꜀ contact is important, and with a larger group the
scale of applying it is larger too, but the principle is
identical

•⟩⟩ Be yourself. This is important for any presentation. You
may want to exaggerate a little, and an expansive gesture
may need to be that little more expansive in a packed
conference room, but do not change your basic style
because of the numbers. It is easier for you to be natural
and the impression given is better for the audience, all of
them

•⟩⟩ Use feedback. If there are more people there will be more
of it, somewhere in the audience there will be an
enthusiastic response to focus on

•⟩⟩ Use involvement. Of course, the appropriate level of
formality varies, but there is no real reason not to say:
What do you think about this? and prompt a comment or
three from an audience of a hundred than there is from
one of a dozen. Similarly you can focus on individuals
even in a crowd if that is appropriate: *John Black is here
somewhere – where are you John? And what do you think?*
– especially if they will appreciate it

•⟩⟩ Do not let sheer numbers put you off anything that the
presentation needs, for example if you need to
pause......pause, do not let the pressure of many eyes
make you spoil what may be an important emphasis

•⟩⟩ Think of the total audience in sub-section, use eye
contact to focus on small groups within the audience,
then pretend to yourself that you are talking to just the
six at the back or the three in the front row.

Of course, you need to double-check certain things carefully with a large group (for example, the microphone or the acoustics), otherwise relax and do not let it worry you. It is, in any case, the kind of thing that usually proves more worrying before you do it, than it does while you are doing it. If you present appropriately to the subject, the occasion and the audience, then the number present need not change things greatly. Everyone in any group is an individual. Talk to them as individuals and there is no reason why they should not all be satisfied.

Organising the environment

By this I mean not Green issues, but the speaking environment, the room and particularly the immediate area you inhabit at the front of the room. If you work to ensure you are comfortable with all the arrangements that affect you, there is at once much less to distract your mind as you speak; all your thoughts can then focus on the job in hand. If not …. well imagine some of the hazards of this sort:

The table in front of you is narrow. It has an overhead projector of some sort standing firmly in its centre, and there is little room for your notes and slides. There is no time to reorganise the layout, so you perch your papers on a corner, and begin to place used overhead projector slides on a chair a little to one side. You are well prepared in most ways but your mind constantly flits from one hazard to the next: are your papers safe? Are you reaching far enough to put things safely on the chair? Have you remembered exactly where the curling electric wire connecting the projector to the power main lies? Why is the water jug perched on a saucer two sizes too small and why, like so many jugs, will it not pour without cascading ice cubes far and wide?

At the same time you attempt to keep small portions of your mind on the time, maintain eye contact with members of the group and …. your foot catches – just slightly – the electric cable, enough to move the projector an inch or two to one side and knock the water jug …

But I am sure that your own imagination can no doubt do better (or worse?). None of this should happen. Creating the right environment needs thought and planning, and the precise arrangement will depend on the circumstances and such things as whether there is a lectern, but you can and should create an arrangement as near to your ideal as any individual situation allows. Several aspects of thinking and action are necessary or desirable here:

First, prior selection and arrangement of key physical factors

- •)) Whether you want to use a lectern or not

- •)) Equipment in the right place (projector, flipchart or anything else that may be involved)

- •)) Equipment tested and working

- •)) Hazards removed or taped down: as with electric wires

- •)) Water jug and glass standing in a safe place

- •)) Sufficient space for all you want to do (lay out notes, slides and so on)

- •)) Acoustics checked (finding out how loud to speak has been mentioned).

The above factors are basic; more may occur to you and others may be necessary in special circumstances. For instance, is there a clock you can see? (If not, you may want to take off your wristwatch and lay it in front of you to avoid looking visibly – pointedly – at it on your wrist.) Can you easily see any necessary signals from the Chair? Can you signal to anyone necessary (someone at the back who will summon the refreshments)?

Another thing that may need organising is a microphone. It is not always necessary, but if you must use one then always test it to see not only that the audience will be able to hear, but that you know how loud you need to speak (you should not have to raise your voice unnaturally, but it should accommodate a louder tone if you need this for emphasis). The most difficult thing about microphones is remembering to stay the right distance from them; only practise really helps here. The problem often does not occur these days as you can have a tiny microphone clipped to your lapel, connected to a radio device that goes in your pocket or on your belt. If this is positioned correctly then you can just forget about it.

It may be worth your making a short checklist of the things that are important to the kind of presentation you have to make, and the location(s) in which you usually find yourself conducting them.

Note: certain things need organising differently depending on whether one is left or right-handed. To work an OHP neatly, being right-handed, I need to stand to the left of it (as I face it). This is one factor to watch out for, especially if you are at an outside venue. In twenty or more years of working regularly in hotels where many of my courses are accommodated, I have only been asked once by the hotel staff whether I am right or left-handed and often equipment is set up inappropriately. PowerPoint operation is similarly affected.

•)) *What suits you:* by this I mean not just things which you
   personally find create comfort for you (it does not matter
   if others are left cold by them) but that you just *like* –
   what you might think of as personal comfort factors. For
   example, I find I speak regularly from behind a standard
   height table. Fine, one of reasonable width usually gives
   plenty of room for notes, slides, projector and more. But
   if I lay any notes I have flat on the table then I cannot see
   them clearly if they are in standard-sized type. I wear
   spectacles and have found that if I lay a good-sized, hard
   briefcase on the table and put notes on that, just four to
   six inches higher, then I can focus at a glance and, from
   the perspective of the audience, do not appear to be
   looking down so much. It suits me, looks fine and is easy
   to arrange.

Such personal 'likes' can become something of a personal fetish. You *must* have certain things just right to be a hundred per cent comfortable. Clearly if this feeling gets too strong it could become a problem. When you do not have complete control of everything, and if sometimes conditions are not ideal, you do not want this to throw you. On the other hand, I think perhaps that if you are inclined to nerves, it is actually useful to invent a few such things; then organising them your way gives a small but useful feeling of satisfaction and you can start off feeling you are, in a sense, on familiar ground.

As a further point here, note that going into an unfamiliar room just before you speak is to be avoided if possible. What you have perhaps assumed is that it will be a well-equipped meeting room, yet it turns out to be the very opposite and you find yourself in less than ideal circumstances and with no time to correct them. If it is your meeting there is less of a problem (and no excuse for not checking); if you are a guest never be afraid to raise issues in advance with the Chair or organiser. This can be done at any time: in a phone call days before the event, or face to face a few minutes before the event starts. They are normally only too happy to make some small changes if doing this will make you more comfortable.

Finally, always be flexible and take whatever action you can to allow yourself to adapt to varying conditions. For example, as I have said, I often find myself speaking from a normal height table. I tend to have notes in a ring binder and place this on a thick hard briefcase. However, if I assume this and find I am at a small lectern, with no room for the binder, or simply have to stand up out in the open, I always have a solid card in my folder and a bulldog clip – I can take out the notes, arrange them as it were on a clipboard and stand holding them safely in one hand. Again preparation and practice enables you to develop such solutions based on experience.

Your voice

Another source of concern to some is their voice, or rather the projection of it. Public speaking should not be a strain. If it is then it will show, the audience will hear the strain and may even read it wrongly, believing you to be uncertain perhaps just when you want to sound authoritative.

Again, this should not be a problem. You may feel your voice is inadequate to the task, but it almost certainly will do the job supremely well. As an actress friend Constance Lamb once said to me: listen to children in the playground. They all have huge voices, seemingly endless lung capacity and projecting their voice causes them no problem at all (and if you live down the road from a school, you will know!). Why should that ability change with age? If it does then it is because the wrong habits build up. The solution is relaxation and breathing.

Here I will plunder my friend's views again. I asked her what the key factors here are; she told me:

Most people do not breathe properly when they speak. The breath supports the voice and has plenty of power and energy. If you speak on the 'held' breath, this creates tension and stress in the voice and blocks off the power. You will create the best impact by speaking on the outward breath, by using the diaphragm – the muscle that can best be described as the 'kicker', and which propels the breath and the voice outwards. Only in this way can an actor use their voice to fill a large theatre, and it also helps control nerves. If the technique will cope with that then no presenter should have a great problem.

It is easy to demonstrate this to yourself. If you receive a shock, you automatically breathe in sharply by contracting the diaphragm, then 'hold' the breath without letting go. Try it. Take a sharp breath. Hold it. You will find that some tension soon starts to creep in. Now breathe out with a big, audible sigh. The diaphragm relaxes and the tension vanishes. Often everyday speech happens on the held breath, and the breath is only released after completing a sentence.

The best way to project is to speak during the exhalation of a breath. Try it. Notice the difference. Proper breathing – in slowly through the mouth, expanding the rib cage front, back and sides – imagine the rib cage is like a bellows – is the only way to obtain sufficient air when speaking. It fills the lungs fully and easily. And fast. Taking a few slow, deep breaths like this before you start a talk, particularly if you consciously relax the shoulders and chest as you do so, will relax you.

With this working well you can concentrate on using your voice to produce the modulation and the emphasis any formal presentation needs. Certain potential problems can be cured simply by the manner in which you speak. For example, a person who habitually speaks too fast has only to articulate words (and especially consonants) and pronounce the endings of words clearly, and the pace slows automatically.

All good advice, and some of these points are picked up again in Chapter 5. Here I would add only one more comment. Men and women have voices of different pitch. This means that straining is more clearly audible in a woman whose voice will quickly become squeaky if forced. It may be that some women need to intentionally pitch their voice just a little lower than they would in normal conversation.

The voice is the vehicle for your messages, and to attempt to make presentations with no conscious thought of it is akin to setting out on a car journey without checking the petrol gauge.

Finally, let me link again all that has been said in this chapter back to preparation. Perhaps the greatest antidote to nerves is to know you are thoroughly and well prepared. If you know what you are going to talk about (and what you will omit), how you are going to go through the message – in detail, the order, where you will exemplify, illustrate or give emphasis – and have related this to the audience to whom you will speak, the timing and other circumstances and have some suitable notes in front of you – then instead of rising to your feet thinking, *I hope this will be all right* you can do so thinking, *I believe this is going to go well.* Having done your homework (as it were) your confidence will rise and outweigh your uncertainties.

A useful analogy here is that of a juggler. They may keep many balls in the air, but often, if things go wrong, they do not drop one but more. The same situation can be imagined in terms of the reach of your mind: if you are trying to speak and simultaneously let your mind worry about a whole raft of possible difficulties, then the possibility of your faltering is high. By organising things as this chapter has suggested you effectively reduce the number of things on which your mind has to focus to manageable proportions. You can then concentrate solely on what you say and how you say it. Realistically there may be some other things to be borne in mind, but they can be kept firmly on the sidelines.

You will maybe never get rid of every last butterfly (perhaps you should not do so, anyway), but you should not have your mind distracted by groundless fears and matters that can be organised away, when you need all your concentration on the main task in hand, that of putting your ideas across effectively.

You may (presently) be unaccustomed to public speaking: but you should never be unprepared.

CHAPTER 3

Be Prepared

It usually takes me three weeks to prepare a good impromptu speech

Mark Twain

Preparation is a grand word for engaging the brain before the mouth. But it is vital. It makes all the difference between a professional presentation and an indifferent one; or, at worst, an awkward and embarrassing experience. It does not just have to be done; it has to be done thoroughly. It has to be done right. Few, if any, such personal skills come down to the application of any one 'magic formula'. Would that life were so simple! With presentations however, preparation must come close – it is crucial to success and should never be skimped.

No-one wants what appears to be a well considered dramatic pause to be a wild groping for what on earth should come next. And it is difficult to concentrate on anything – still less inject some sort of flourish – when some failure of preparation is distracting you from something basic such as what comes next. In this chapter we review some of the key tasks of preparation and the way of going about them. In dissecting the process there is a danger that it appears complex or at least lengthy. The reverse is actually true. A systematic approach makes preparation simpler, and once you build up certain habits you will find that your preparation takes up a more and more manageable time in relation to the duration of the presentation you have to make. First things first – the first task seems simple, but a systematic approach is even helpful in terms of assembling the message.

One point needs to be made firmly at this stage. Preparation does not mean starting at the beginning and writing out what you intend to say from beginning to end verbatim. Even if you did this it might lead to your being tempted to read the text, and this is not likely to make for a good overall effect. There are exceptions to this (when the need for precision demands what is said must have word for word accuracy) but these are not the norm. Besides, reading something aloud with clarity is, in fact, very difficult for most, as it tends to sound stilted and stifle any animation that should be present.

Something that shows this difficulty in a slightly different way is seen day by day as we watch news and current affairs programmes on the television. Politicians often read from tele-prompters: these have a screen on which their pre-written words scroll up at just the right pace for them to read the words. The words appear big and bold and thus there are not so many words to a line as in normal printed material. This can cause a regularly heard fault that dilutes the impact of what they do, one that can be particularly annoying to the listener. They abandon all punctuation, pausing exclusively at the end of each line in a way that bears no relation to the sense of what they are saying. So, you hear something like this:

Good morning, ladies and -

Gentlemen. I am very pleased -

To be here today to speak to you -

About our policy on overseas -

Aid. This is a vital area, one that -

Contributes to Britain's role -

In ...

And so on – and on; the effect is clearly not good. And, at worst, one sometimes finds oneself focusing just on this fault and failing to take in anything that is actually said.

So you should make it a rule: do not write out your presentation in full and do not read it. That said – how do you prepare? A systematic approach is suggested, one that might best be described as moving from the general to the particular, or from outline and key skeleton points to fully fleshed talk. And the starting point is to have a clear idea of your intentions and objective.

A clear intention

Be very clear about what you are going to do (from here on it may be useful to have in mind something you do by way of example as you read further). Do you want to:

- •)) Inform
- •)) Explain or instruct
- •)) Motivate
- •)) Persuade
- •)) Prompt debate
- •)) Demonstrate
- •)) Build on past messages or dialogue with members of the audience?

You may want to do some or all of these, or to add other intentions to the list. The point here is that there may well be several things of this sort to do, and it makes preparation, and delivery, easier if you are clear about them all at the outset. You certainly do not want to be busy informing people and then suddenly think, I really should be enthusing them a bit too. It is difficult to suddenly start to try to address a newly thought of intention half-way through a talk.

This links to the next heading: you need a clear objective.

Setting objectives

Regularly when I run sessions to help improve presentation skills, I find I have participants in the session who, whatever their other strengths or weaknesses, fail to deliver the standard of presentation they want because – and sometimes *solely* because – they do not have clear objectives. They sort of speak *about* something, but without real purpose; without it *really going anywhere.*

Objectives are not what you wish to say, they are what you wish to *achieve* by saying something.

For example, a manager may need to address a staff meeting of some sort about a new policy. The task is almost certainly not simply to tell them about the policy, more likely it is to ensure they understand the change and how it will work, accept the necessity for it and are promptly able to undertake future work in a way that fits the new policy.

Taking such a view of what needs to be done is surely more likely to make preparing a presentation easier and surer. Simplistically we might immediately see such a talk as making five points:

- •)) Some background to the change

- •)) An explanation of why it is necessary (perhaps in terms of the good things it will achieve)

- •)) Exactly what the change is and how it will work

- •)) The effect on the individual

- •)) What action needs to be taken and by when.

If you think of something like a new procedure for handling customer complaints, or any sensitive or complicated issue, then the danger of some detail being omitted or inadequately dealt with (or understood) is at once clear. Given a more precise case, objectives should always be, as a much quoted acronym has it, SMART. That is they should be:

•)) Specific

•)) Measurable

•)) Achievable

•)) Realistic and

•)) Timed.

And they should have a clear focus on the audience. It is more important to think about what will work for them, rather than what it is that *you* want in isolation. Thus, to show how this works, you might regard objectives in this light for your reading of this book as:

•)) To enable you to ensure your future presentations come over in a way that will be seen by their audiences as appropriate and informative *(specific)*

•)) To ensure *(measurable)* action occurs afterwards (for example, the success of certain future presentations might be measured by the number of people agreeing to take certain actions after they have heard them)

•)) Being right for you, providing sufficient information and ideas in a manageable form for you to really be able to make a difference to what you do in future (providing an *achievable* objective)

•)) To be not just achievable – possible – but *realistic*, that is, desirable (for example, here the time it takes to read this book, thus taking you away from other matters, might be compared with the possible gains from so doing – if it took, say, a couple of days this might well be over-engineering)

•)) And *timed* – when are you going to review (in part by reading the book) how you go about making presentations? After all, results cannot come from such a review until it has occurred.

Before you get up and speak you must always be able to answer questions about your talk such as:

- •)) Why am I doing this? (for example, so that people are better informed)

- •)) What am I trying to achieve? (say, to put them in a position to take, willingly and effectively, a particular action).

If you do this and if you find the answer is too unspecific, then the internal conversation needs extending, saying: *which means that* after your first answer and continuing with more explicit descriptions until a real description is found that truly answers the question. So, saying, *This is a talk about time management* is insufficient. It might be interesting, but what are the objectives. If we say, *This is a talk about time management* and extend the thought, *which means that I want people to understand the process, see it as manageable and actually be able to do things afterwards that will improve their productivity* then we are getting a lot clearer and more specific.

The need for clear intentions and objectives is always the same. It may be more obvious in a business context, but it is just as evident for the best man at a wedding who has certain duties to perform (some thanks to give, for example) but should probably also be intending to amuse (suitably!), respect the nature of the occasion and play his part in creating a memorable occasion.

Once that is clear, then the real task of deciding what is to be said can begin and must, as has been said earlier, be carried through systematically, creating a skeleton and then adding the 'flesh' to produce the complete message. See Figure 1, which illustrates this graphically.

Start with a skeleton:	Add the 'flesh'	Complete the total message
Main point	Main point -secondary point -secondary point	Main point - secondary point + example - secondary point
Main point	Main point -secondary point	Main point - secondary point + example - additional point
Main point	Main point -secondary point -secondary point	Main point - secondary point + example - secondary point - additional point
Main point	Main point -secondary point	Main point - secondary point - summary

FIGURE 1: *Putting 'flesh' on the structure*

Deciding what to say

A four-stage approach does the job of composition well, and is likely to make preparation quicker and more certain.

1 Listing

This consists of ignoring any thoughts about sequence or structure and simply listing everything – every point – that it might be desirable or necessary to say something about (perhaps while bearing something about the duration and level of detail involved in mind in order to keep things manageable; after all, being comprehensive is *never* one of the objectives, no talk is *that* long). This simple process gets all the elements involved down on paper. It takes just a minute or two and, for something short, might go on the back of an envelope. Alternatively, it may need more time and more than one session to complete it. A gap in doing so sometimes stimulates the thinking, and certainly you will find one thought leading to another. What results could be simply a list, a column of points going down the page. But I believe you will find it works better in accommodating the developing picture to adopt a 'freestyle' approach, as shown in Figure 2 opposite.

This freestyle approach is to be recommended as it makes it easier to encapsulate content. Rather than write a list (which tends to prompt you to think sequentially) the best starting point is to note all the possible topics/points 'freestyle' around the page in a way that is free from any worry about detail such as what comes first, second and so on. The example here, albeit with the detail abbreviated somewhat to make things clearer, imagines the first part of a short presentation about the need for effective time management (something I have written about in *Successful Time Management* [Kogan Page]) to illustrate the idea:

When this is done you can proceed to the next stage.

What is time management?   common prevailing
                                                    attitudes/practice

You need
  a plan   Results of good time management:
                improved - productivity
                         - quality
                         - efficiency
                         - creativity
                Bad : all above are reduced + stress/hassle etc.
                                                    increase

career link

                    80/20 rule   meetings

      Bad news/good news → difficult → detail + habit

      timewasters

      cumulative effect of small changes (e.g. numbers)

                        getting/staying organised

      setting priorities - link to job objective

            examples of controlling time wasters

concept of investing   Action →
  time to save time

FIGURE 2: *Example of 'freestyle' approach to this stage of preparation*

2 Sorting

Next you can proceed to rearrange what you have written more logically, deciding and recording the sequence in which you will take things and how things relate one to another. This may raise new questions as well as resolve others, so is still not a final structure. You might best undertake such initial rearrangement simply by annotating the original list to clarify how matters will be dealt with (a second colour is useful to do this simply). Figure 3 continues the example started previously, though you must imagine the second colour and the full arrangement. The four key actions here are to:

- •)) Decide and note the running order

- •)) Link thoughts and topics that fit together

- •)) Delete things felt to be inappropriate or which go into too much detail

- •)) Add anything overlooked and necessary.

As you do this the amount of detail you can begin to put in will vary. It may be that you will add a good deal of detail, with some of it in the form of exact words. For example, in talking about time management I sometimes quote something I read in an American book: *They didn't want it right, they wanted it Wednesday.* To ensure that I can quote that correctly I might well note it down in full. In other places it might be that one word is sufficient to prompt several minutes of a talk.

In doing this 'sorting' you may not only have to think logically, though this is important: you need to explain things or make points in an order that makes sense. It may be that the structure can contribute more, indeed the structure can link to how you give the whole speech a theme and a tone that is part of what makes it work.

Because this overlaps with content it maybe that it must be done in parallel with deciding about content. Perhaps I may illustrate this with a personal example. Although I speak regularly in a business

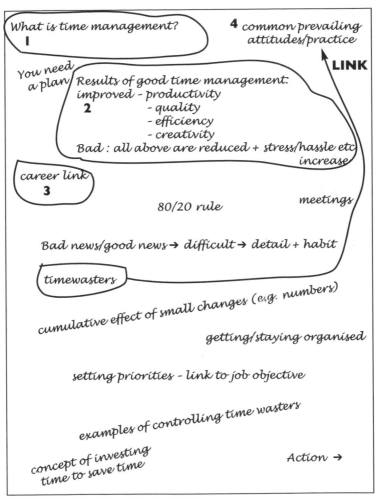

FIGURE 3: *Sorting: example of this stage of preparation*

context, a big social occasion needs different approaches. When my daughter was married not so long ago the thought of making the 'father of the bride speech' was totally unfamiliar to me, and initially a bit scary. I found that the main problem was that I was unsure how to set about it without a theme. I looked up a book on wedding speeches to discover exactly what the father of the bride was supposed to do (talk about my daughter, welcome her new husband to the family and so on). I then prepared the speech in sections, and based it on a fictional guide, which I called jokingly 'Ptolemy's top tips for timid toast givers'. This allowed an amusing lead in to each section and, once decided upon, made my preparation very much easier. By imposing a theme and arrangement on it I made it manageable: a specific number of short sections had to be prepared and then linked neatly together; this, I found, made the whole process easier. I am told it worked well on the day, too.

Next, the example of the previous boxed paragraph, showing the annotation that might be added at this stage, can be further refined.

3 Arranging

Only now do you add (or redraft as your jottings may have become untidy and difficult to follow) the sequence and precise arrangement of the topic. Here the general principles are shown: the detail of exactly how you should view the structure of a talk forms the thread to the next chapter. This can be simply presented – see Figure 4 – or be elaborated into the final form of whatever style of 'speaker's notes' for which you opt (something we come to in detail shortly). If you opt for a neat list here, then this may be the time to type it up and print it out from your computer. Such notes can begin to add a note of any emphasis necessary in presenting the material – anything from a dramatic pause to a raised voice, or a point repeated for emphasis – or this can wait until you turn your notes into actual speaker's notes suitable to have in front of you on the day. Here we concentrate on assembling the content of the message-to-be, as it were.

Note: two points are worth a special mention here:

- •)) Although a common fear of the inexperienced is that you will not have sufficient material, more often the reverse is true, and a common fault is trying to squeeze in too much, resulting in a rushed rather that a measured delivery and an audience missing much of what is there, or worse, becoming confused

•)) This limit on quantity is particularly true of individual points – there should not be too many – and the key skeleton of key points, and sub-points, should stand out and be manageable within the total material.

TIME MANAGEMENT

Common problem - results : less (productivity etc.)/more (stress, hassle etc.)

Makes a difference to job/career

Fact of life : 80/20 rule - 20% of your time produces 80% of results

What makes it difficult (no magic formula/ success in detail)

What makes it easier: establishing habits

You need a plan - and a diary system

Deciding priorities

Controlling timewasters: you and others (and meetings)

Action for the future

FIGURE 4: *Arranging: example of this stage of preparation*

It is difficult to suggest a rule of thumb here. It is clearly dangerous to leave out a key element of an argument, but time is at a premium for most of us these days and succinctness is often either appreciated, or essential. Many presenters may be given a time – *I want you to present this to the Board; just ten minutes mind.* Having a clear structure allows you to be sure the content is appropriate, and matching that to the audience and to time restraints will help you make a final decision about what you can and should do. If in doubt it is probably better to limit points rather than confuse your audience with sheer quantity; leaving people wanting more may be better than boring them to death with seemingly endless minute detail.

Note: when time is limited this may need to be referred to specifically. In other words, as you tell people what you will do you make it clear that what is possible, especially in terms of the level of detail you will go into, is designed – perhaps restricted – by the time you are allocated. You do not want people to assume you have no restrictions when you have, and it may be better for people to regard you as having done a good job in the time available, rather than thinking you should have expanded on things when that was not possible.

At this stage you have the rough notes of the listing and sorting stages rewritten in an ordered form, which can be subject to final review as necessary.

Note: this then becomes the main skeleton in terms of structure and content, dividing into a beginning, middle and end, and being fleshed out and turned into your own form of running notes to provide the level of detail required.

4 Review

Finally, ahead of actually setting things out in a form that works as a guide while you speak, you need to review what you have done. It is no reflection on your abilities if it is not to your complete satisfaction first time. Many people need to work over material several times to get it right, though experience will limit this process. At this stage it may suffice to check over what is down on paper in your mind, though you can usefully go further and rehearse – a stage better done once you have your 'speaker's notes' to hand and one to which we return.

This final review stage is important and can quickly fine-tune material into something that is not simply a sound message, but one arranged so that it can be effectively delivered.

A bear of very little brain

There is one factor here that should be spelt out clearly, one advantage of this sort of systematic approach, which, for most people, is a great help. I like to think I am reasonably adept at many things, but I also know that if I try to do, or concentrate on, too much at once I become muddled. What the systematic approach to preparation does is to separate two key, yet different tasks: it means that you concentrate first on the content, *what* you will say, and only secondly as you go through the process on *how* you will put it over. Maybe I am a simple soul, but I find that easier than simply looking at what I must do sequentially and trying to work out what I need to say and how I can best put it at the same time. If it is easier to work this way, it is likely to be quicker to prepare also. Better speeches in less time seem like good reasons for going about the preparation process in a systematic way.

The detail about making the presentation reviewed later will reinforce the need for careful preparation. There is a good deal to think about. But there is no reason why, with practice, the process of assembling a talk should not be accomplished in a reasonable amount of time. However, to begin with at least, it should not be skimped. There is a good deal to think about, and even a short talk demands care and attention. Some would say that one should say *especially* a short talk, and certainly in a few short minutes any faults will stand out sharply and small details can have a disproportionate impact for both good and ill; but I digress.

Next we turn to the main manifestation of this preparation: *speaker's notes*. Few of us can sustain a well-organised talk without some written detail in front of us (though practice or repetition may allow you to reduce this in some instances to a few key words). Some people, who impress by speaking apparently without notes, may well still have a few notes on cards safe in their pocket just in case they need them. Initially having something thought through that really suits you is vital, but it cannot be any old series of jottings. It must be tailored to its use – on your feet.

Speaker's notes

Having something clear and simple to follow as a guide boosts confidence, it acts like a firm hand on the tiller, assisting you to maintain direction and aiding control (and also facilitating digression where that may be appropriate). As has been said earlier, the trick is not to write out the speech verbatim, rather to reflect the skeleton of the material, prompt particular factors – from moments of emphasis, such as a dramatic pause, to using a visual of some sort – and to remind you of the detail against the background of a clear structure.

It is worth evolving a specific format that suits *you*. There is no need to follow anyone else's ideas unless they suit – though take what is useful from wherever you come across it. If you use the same broad approach consistently it speeds preparation, and assists monitoring time as you get to know how long a page or card in your personal style represents in terms of delivery time.

The following comments spell out a complete format suggestion in some detail. You may want to use all, or most, of this initially, but of course you can also use – or move onto – a simplified version of it. As has been said, it is what suits you that matters, but be sure that omitting some element of guidance does not make what you do on your feet any less certain. What follows is designed to help you develop such a style.

Some practical points first:

- •)) Notes must be legible (use a sufficiently large size of typeface or writing), and legible not just as would be right sitting at your desk, but when on your feet

- •)) Ensure notes will stay flat as you use them on the day (an A4 ring binder may be best, or cards loosely linked with a tie-cord)

- •)) Using only one side of the paper allows amendment and addition if necessary (or if you are using a fair number of slides then a copy of these might go alongside your notes)

•)) *Always* number the pages – you do not want to get lost (and you would not be the first to drop your notes if disaster strikes). Some people like doing the numbering in reverse, with the last page being number one – the countdown effect acts to provide information about how much material and time you have left in front of you as you proceed

•)) Separate graphically different kinds of instruction and material (for example, making clear *what* you will say and also indicating something about *how* you will say it)

•)) Use colour and symbols to provide emphasis.

For example, imagine first a small segment of a talk about time management as it would be spoken in full. Here is a possible extract discussing the base problem posed:

> *So, we all need to manage time effectively. We all have our work constantly interrupted – for example a manager may find people constantly at their door saying something like, 'What do I do about this?'. Tell them and you guarantee an endless chain of interruptions - more of this anon. Yet there are inherent difficulties involved. The English classic author G K Chesterton said, about the decline of religion, that it was not that it had been tried and found wanting, it was that it had been found difficult and therefore not tried. Few people are perfect time managers. But what makes a difficult task easier? The key is adopting the right attitude towards the process, seeing it as something to work at, one where there may be no one magic formula but where the details matter, and the time implications of everything must be considered.*

> *Not easy: but a conscious effort to change can ensure good practice quickly becomes habit; and thus that things get progressively easier.*

> *Every piece of time saved is valuable, and adds up. Years*

ago, in the theatrical revue 'Beyond the Fringe', a British Prime Minister was mocked, commenting on the four-minute warning (the time between the Russians launching a nuclear attack and annihilation). He was portrayed as saying , 'Some people in this great country of ours can run a mile in four minutes'. Not long given the circumstances, but save four minutes every day and you will have more than two extra days of working time in a year. I could use that – and so, I bet, could you. So, what can we do?

And so on, but this should provide enough for our purposes.

With these actual spoken words in mind, consider what might have been down on the page to create them. This is shown below. The detail here will be sufficient to give any speaker – who is otherwise well prepared – something easy to follow. The grey tint represents the bright colour of a highlighter pen (use your imagination!). Certainly colour makes a difference to the clarity of these sorts of notes and can be used in numbers of ways: if, as well as such highlighting, underlining, bullet points, certain words, symbols and maybe more stand out in, say, red, it does help. In this way the eye can quickly focus on each element without too much conscious effort.

Figure 5, which charts one part of the time management talk, uses a number of particular ideas you may be able to copy or adapt, viz:

- •)) The page is ruled (use colour here) into two smaller blocks that are each of a size that is easier to focus on as you look to and fro from the audience to the page (remember this example represents an A4 page, though its content could equally be spread over 2/3 cards)

- •)) Symbols are used (for example, to show here there is a slide to put on or a need to pause). Always use the same symbol for the same thing or you may find yourself puzzling over what they mean

- •)) Columns are used to separate main headings from the body of the notes and leave room for additional material

Time: 10 minutes		
It's difficult	GKC " - not tried and found wanting, found difficult and therefore not tried." ! You? _ _ _ * Problems - interruptions No magic formula ⟶ ⟶ * What makes it possible? - Detail - Habit but realistically: never perfect but worthwhile.	OPTIONS e.g. Members of team / lack confidence / always seeking advice
What can be gained?	* Beyond Fringe story (S4) 4 minutes over a year [list of points]	

Key:

(S6) Show sixth slide

* Always precedes key points

⤳ Links

! For emphasis

_ _ _ _ Pause

[≡] List of points

FIGURE 5: *Speaker's notes: format example*

•))) Emphasis is shown (again colour does this best)

•))) Text is spaced out (to allow further amendment and make it easier to focus on)

•))) Timing is mentioned (this can repeat through the piece)

Each page is numbered

•))) There are *'options'* that can be used, or not, as time and circumstances allow, something that can be very useful to both timing and fine-tuning perhaps in the light of an audience's reaction. The idea here is that the main content and, say, half the options will give you the duration you want. You then decide as you go along which of these to use. Such 'options' can be a valuable device, and inject a considerable element of flexibility into what you do; it helps you keep to time and maximise the impact you make.

Remember you should think carefully about what suits you best and evolve a personal style that works for you. It is worth a little experiment to achieve this. The end result can be typed, or handwritten, or be a mixture of both.

The notes you use represents an area well worth thinking about, and experimenting with. You will find that if you decide on a style of reminder note that really suits you, it will provide a real asset to you forevermore. Your style may evolve over time, of course. You may have different versions of it for differing purposes, and the amount of detail you record may be different depending on such factors as how well you know the topic on which you must speak, or the precise duration involved. Whatever you decide, your system can always act as a sure foundation for what you have to do and its very familiarity will, in time, become a part of its usefulness.

From first thoughts to spoken word

As an example of how the thinking can be done, let me focus on the start of a talk about time management. At first what needs to be said may be clear only in outline:

•)) There is a need for good time management – it is worthwhile – it can be achieved – it just needs a realistic approach.

How is this to be explained? Next some detail is added:

•)) There is a need for good time management (the pressure and stress of the modern workplace/ what good time management improves/ what bad time management makes worse) – it is worthwhile (with care you really can be more productive) – it can be achieved (it is not easy/ there are factors that help) – it just needs a realistic approach (you need a plan).

This is a factual piece and the actual content is beginning to come together, but how will it best be said? As people are often poor at time management it needs to be made accessible. Again the initial thoughts are expanded:

•)) Needs a challenging start – there is a need for good time management (the pressure and stress of the modern workplace/ what good time management improves/ what bad time management makes worse)

•)) Needs specific factors highlighting – it is worthwhile (with care you really can be more productive)

•)) Needs a way of illustrating this – it can be achieved (it is not easy/ there are factors that help)

•)) Both factors need spelling out and what assists need emphasis) – it just needs a realistic approach (you need a plan)

•)) But one that is straightforward and not itself time consuming.

Add an element or two to inject more life: a quotation perhaps, maybe a lighter touch, and it is close to how it can be said. The speaker's note will highlight the content, sequence, and something of the way it is said. On the day it might sound something like this (skipping any necessary introductions and starting with the real beginning on the topic):

'How many of us have too much to do and not enough time? Most of us, I suspect. The workplace seems to get busier and more stressful as you watch, and we all contend with targets, deadlines and a thousand and one things that seem to conspire to make life difficult.

Yet some people seem to stay on top of things. Poor time management can reduce productivity, and efficiency and jeopardise quality standards and creativity. On the other hand, good time management can improve all of these and see things achieved with less – perhaps no – hassle or stress, and without constant wheel reinvention. It is a skill that benefits what we do in our jobs – and how we progress in our careers.

The bad news is that achieving good time management is not easy. The English classic author G K Chesterton wrote, about the decline of religion, that the reason for that was ... *not that it had been tried and found wanting, but that it had been found difficult and therefore not tried.* So it is too with time management. Too many of us – overpowered by pressure and constant interruptions – see the situation as something uncontrollable. We battle on, but fail to take any action that can really make a permanent difference.

While there is no magic formula, no one thing we can do that will change everything at a stroke, there are a lot of ways to improve things – the solution is in the details. The good news is that we can develop good habits so that good time management becomes a reflex. It is worthwhile too. Some of you may remember, way back – in the days when sex was safe and the Russians were dangerous – Peter Cook speaking as the Prime Minister in the review *'Beyond the Fringe'*. Challenged about the threat of nuclear attack and the four-minute warning he said, *Some people in this great country of ours can run a mile in four minutes.* Not much help if the bomb is going off perhaps – but just think about four minutes for a moment.

In a typical working year, if you save four minutes every day you will have more than two extra days to work with – four minutes may not sound much, but two extra days I for one could certainly do with! And if there are numerous ways in which we can save time the rewards in terms of 'new' time mount up very usefully.

How do we go about improving our management of time? First we need a plan ...'

Of course there is no one right way of saying this, and how it is said must relate to a number of other factors: the nature of the audience, the duration allowed for the whole talk, and more. But the progression here is clear. Given a clear intention – here to prompt people to think about the subject and take action to improve work practices – it is easiest and most effective to start with the bare outline and add content to build towards what you want, going into more or less detail as may be appropriate and matching the final way something is delivered to the occasion.

Rehearsal

Once you have what you aim to say planned, and documented in a form that you can refer to and speak from 'on the day', you may want to move from just thinking about and planning what you intend to do to actually trying it out – rehearsing. This too may be done in your head, but may usefully involve talking through the final form out loud, or recording it on a tape recorder (or dictating machine). While it may be sufficient to practise to the bathroom mirror, it may be better to have a trial run through with a sympathetic friend or colleague listening (although, on second thoughts, you may think it prudent to omit the 'sympathetic'; some constructive criticism and ideas may well help, although you must ultimately decide the final form). Within an organisation you might do this on a swap basis. It takes some time, but if you have a colleague who can do it for you from time to time in return for your doing it for them it is fair – and useful to both of you. For anything especially important, this is a stage well worth giving some time to – not least, a complete run through, however it may be done, is the only certain way to judge whether the duration is going to be as you want it to be, at least until experience makes that judgement easier.

Do not rule these ideas out because they may seem embarrassing, even talking to a recorder in an empty room may seem odd and awkward, but rehearsal can really help, especially at a stage when your experience is still limited.

With a little help from your friends

Before leaving the subject of preparation, there is the matter of team presentations to be touched on. When a complete presentation is made up of segments with perhaps two, three or more people contributing separate parts of it, the need for preparation is magnified. Team presentations must not only go over well, they must also appear seamless. There should be neither any disruption to the smooth flow of the content, nor any fumbling in terms of handover between speakers. Those in the audience will read any uncertainty as unprofessional. It will seem to be either a sign of bad planning or appear as a lack of respect for the audience – or both. Even if the individual presentations are good, any fumbling on handover – *I think that's all I have to say. John, you were going to pick things up here, weren't you?* – will dilute effectiveness.

It is often extremely difficult for a group of people to present effectively together without getting together beforehand to thrash out the details. Time and pressures within many an organisation may typically conspire to make such meetings difficult to arrange, but there is no substitute for them. A word or two on the telephone or a couple of e-mails is just not the same, and you fail to liaise in this way at your peril. You have been warned.

You need to consider such matters as:

- •)) What order people will speak in (and whether this in any way should relate to the hierarchy involved, often it should not)

- •)) Who will be 'in charge'

- •)) How speaking styles will match or detract

- •)) Who will organise and take questions

- •)) The implications for the timing.

You may think of more.

It is worth a moment. The effect of a seamless ultimate presentation is powerful. It is no fun getting up to speak less well prepared than you know you should be; getting up alongside a colleague having little idea how well what the two of you have to say will mesh together runs a poor second.

A final thought

Most, if not all, of the problems you may anticipate in speaking formally can be removed or reduced by preparation.

Preparation can quite literally make the difference between success and failure, and can turn something routine into something memorable.

Psychologists say that more than seventy per cent of what is called 'self-talk' about speaking formally is negative. This means all those thoughts that start: *I'm not sure I can* ... or *It won't be* ... You need to combat this by thinking positively. Imagine it going well. Visualise the detail of particular elements working as you planned. Why not imagine the applause too? Doubts might otherwise become a self-fulfilling prophecy.

The time for this thinking is as you prepare. And bear in mind that the single most common reason why things sometimes do not go well is because the person concerned gave insufficient time to preparation. Bear in mind too that, quite simply, what you do in preparing creates the certainty that it *will* go well.

So the rule should be: Prepare – Practise – Present.

And, something more ...

Set time aside to – *Excuse me, I'm just – well, just a minute*

Now, yes – set aside time to – *Sorry to interrupt but –*

Where was I? Ah, yes, a final rule:

Try to set aside time to prepare or rehearse uninterrupted. It makes for a quicker and more certain job in the end. Something done piecemeal will simply make creating a fluid whole more difficult.

Now, well prepared and with your notes ready you can consider the detail of exactly how you will put the material across.

Chapter 4

Putting it Over

Speeches are like babies – easy to conceive but hard to deliver

Pat O'Malley

Presentations should have a beginning, a middle and an end. The oldest, and perhaps the wisest, saying about the nature of communications generally is perhaps the advice to: Tell 'em, tell 'em and tell 'em. In other words you should:

- •)) Tell people what you are going to tell them

- •)) Tell them

- •)) And then tell them what you have told them.

It is the way, for instance, a good written report is arranged: an introduction, the body of the content and a summary. If this sounds common sense, it is. It is also an area of common fault. I regularly see people who in other ways are good presenters, diluting the impression they make because they are following no clear structure. They ramble from one thing to the next, constantly saying things like, *And also ..*, *Let me add…*, and, at worst appearing to make up what they say at random as they go along. Their audience gets lost or finds what is being said difficult to follow. The speaker ends up being less impressive than they would have been if they had followed such a structure. Bear in mind the fact that people like to have things in context and know, at least to some extent, what is coming; they also like to find that what is said flows logically.

So, practising what I preach I will link that thought to another and say, briefly, how this chapter is arranged. First, it is no good having a structure if people are unaware of it, so the topic of what is called *signposting* is dealt with next. This leads us to some thoughts about the *audience* – the group to whom everything discussed in this book is ultimately directed. Then the stages – beginning, middle and end – are reviewed in turn to investigate both how they can be made to form a cohesive whole, and also how the detailed way they are handled can make them successful in putting your ideas over.

First then, let me turn back to signposting.

Pointing the way

The technique of *signposting* (or, as it is sometimes called, *labelling*) is something that can be used throughout the presentation process. As people like knowing broadly what they are in for, and appreciate – albeit perhaps subconsciously – help in keeping everything well ordered and in context as you speak, then this is an important technique in carrying a group with you. Indeed, it virtually cannot be overdone. It consists simply of telling people, in outline or in brief, not only what is coming next, but sometimes the purpose or texture of it as well.

It can start with the whole talk. You spell out what is, in effect, an agenda. Thus in talking about a project of some sort, you might say: *Today I want to review three key issues. First, what needs to be done, second, who will do what, and third, the timing involved …*

If the presentation is of any length or complexity, then a similar technique can precede and lead into sub-points: *Now secondly, I said I would discuss the audience; here I want to mention two main, and different, perspectives – what they expect and what they need. First, audience expectations …* Exactly the same sort of process may be relevant down several layers. One point, and something I know I must watch; you need to keep count. I am apt to say, authoritatively: *There are four key issues here,* and when I am up to six, someone in the audience will take delight in pointing out that I cannot count (I reply that I *can* count and it is my creativity that is providing the additional key points, but it is still best not to do this).

This is not simply a convenient device to keep yourself organised, though it does have that effect. People like it. They like to have things in context, know clearly how one thing links to another and know – in advance – something about what is coming next. Similarly you can flag or label the exact nature of particular things you say.

- •)) **Specifically:** *Now let me give you an example:* an example is coming

- •)) **By implication:** *For instance ...:* there is probably an example coming

- •)) **With added meaning:** *This is an odd way of looking at it, but it makes a point ...:* an example is probably coming and it is not a routine one, might even be amusing

- •)) **With added content:** *Consider this in relation to, for instance, an elephant ...:* an example coming up extends the content to a new, and perhaps, unexpected area

- •)) **With an obvious flourish:** *You may think that's irrelevant. In fact it's not an elephant, it's a hippopotamus ...:* the example is used as a pace-breaking aside with a touch of humour (well, when my children were young we all thought it was funny).

In this way the wording you use can signpost intention in all sorts of ways. For instance, you can prompt people to:

- •)) Pay particular attention to a complex point

- •)) Relax

- •)) Relate what is being said to their experience in some way

- •)) Link what is being said now to an earlier point

- •)) Answer (a perhaps rhetorical) question that you will soon pose.

It can get them thinking along particular lines, adding elements of their own experience to support an argument, or just prompt them to file away one point and turn their mind to consideration of the next. With that in mind, consider (signpost!) what the audience want.

The audience

As has been said earlier, the audience want it all to go well. But they are not totally forgiving and they will have expectations: above all they want you to talk *to* them or discuss *with them*, not to talk at them. So keeping the audience viewpoint in mind is, like preparation, another near 'magic' formula for success. It is one that should, of course, affect your preparation as well as your delivery and manner.

Any audience faced with being on the receiving end of a formal talk thinks ahead – a process that may perhaps be coloured by experience of bad or boring presentations they have attended in the past. They try to guess what it will be like. They wonder if it will be interesting, amusing, or useful: or just short. Whatever the intention is, they wonder if it will be achieved. They look for clues to what it will be like even before you start, which is why things like appearance, starting on time, being seen to be organised and comfortable with the proceedings are all important. In training for instance, people are asking questions such as: does this person know their subject? Will they be able to put it over? And will they do so in an interesting manner, and, if they do, will it help me? Each member of a group is an individual, they are concerned above all with themselves, and the good speaker appears to address individuals and not some amorphous entity called 'the audience'.

More specifically, *they want* you to:

- •)) 'Know your stuff'
- •)) Look the part
- •)) Respect them and acknowledge their situation and views

•)) Make what you say link to what they want from the talk

•)) Give them sufficient information to make a considered judgement about what you say (they will weigh up your views, especially if they are going to be required to take some action at the end or after you finish speaking)

•)) Make them understand by the time you finish what that action, if any, is needed or expected of them.

Above all, they want to find what is said: *understandable, interesting* and *a good fit* with the audience and the occasion.

Conversely, *they do not want* to be:

•)) Confused

•)) Blinded with science, technicalities or jargon

•)) Lost in an overcomplicated structure (or lack of one)

•)) Talked down to

•)) Made to struggle to understand inappropriate language

•)) Made to make an enormous jump to relate what is said to their own circumstance.

And they certainly do not want to listen to someone whose lack of preparation makes it clear that they have no respect for the group.

You have to earn the audience's attention. You must create a belief in your credentials for talking to them, create a rapport between yourself and the group, make them want to listen and understand – yet perhaps also keep an open mind throughout about what is still to come. Presentation is aided by a healthy amount of empathy on the part of the speaker and you can do a lot worse than think long and hard about any audience you are due to address; the more you know about them the better, and some prior checking is sometimes advisable. If you expect the group to be very different, in age or experience say, from what is in fact the case, there is a strong likelihood that some at least of what you say to them will fall on stony ground.

I remember once agreeing to give a talk about careers in business to a school and finding myself in front of over a hundred sixth formers – all girls. At one point talking about marketing and trying to describe the creativity involved in something like advertising, I quoted a 'Sale' sign seen in the window of an outdoor and camping shop in Shakespeare's home town of Stratford upon Avon. It said, both descriptively and cleverly, I thought: *Now is the discount of our winter tents*. Previous experience with adult audiences suggested that this would make a good point and raise a smile. At the school: not a flicker. I do not think a single person in the room (except the teacher) recognised the quotation. Sad perhaps, and I certainly had not anticipated this; but you live and learn.

Now, as indicated, we turn to the overall structure and start, with surely unchallengeable logic, at the beginning.

Getting off to a good start

You cannot overestimate the importance of a good start. Remember the old saying: *first impressions last*. The beginning is the introduction; it must set the scene, state the topic and theme (and maybe the reason for the whole thing) – and do so clearly, *and* begin to get into the 'meat' of the message, and do so without too much delay. But it cannot do this in a vacuum. If must get the group's attention and carry people along – and link into the middle and the main section and message of the talk. And to do all this it must establish some sort of rapport between the speaker and audience, one that must become an acceptable basis for holding the interest on throughout the piece. Consider attention and rapport in turn.

Gaining attention

Two things assist here, your manner and the actual start you make. Your manner must get people saying to themselves: *This should be interesting – I think they know what they are talking about*. Here a confident manner pays dividends. If you look the part and proceed as if you are sure of yourself then they will take it that you are. The assumption is made that you would not be doing the talking if you did not know your stuff. But if you appear hesitant or show any sign of being ill prepared then they will start to worry, and that normal assumption will evaporate, and can be replaced with doubt.

Exactly what you say first is also important. Not so much any formalities (though you could perhaps even turn *Good morning* or *Ladies and gentlemen* into something more grabbing), but the first real statement or point. What this means is that you may effectively need two starts: one that deals with any administration and formalities. And another that is the real start into the meat of what you will say. While the first needs to be engaging and done in a way that prompts acceptance of its necessity, the second is perhaps even more important. Some examples of opening techniques you might consider using include:

- •)) **News:** something you know they do not know (and will want to): *Gentlemen, we have hit the target. I heard just as I came into the meeting, and …*

- •)) **Not a lot of people know:** a startling or weird fact: *The next generation of computers, being made now in Japan, can perform ten quadrillion calculations every second.* A quadrillion, incidentally, is a number followed by 18 noughts. That is true, but the same effect might be obtained with something spoof: *There are two kinds of people in the world, those that divide people into categories, and the rest*

- •)) **A question:** actual or rhetorical and ideally designed to get people responding (at least in their minds): *How would you like to …?*

- •)) **A quotation:** whether famous or what a member of the group said yesterday, if it makes a point, generates a smile or links firmly to the topic this can work well: *It was Oscar Wilde who said: 'There is only one thing in the world worse than being talked about, and that is not being* *talked about'* (used to introduce the public relations plan, perhaps)

•)) **A story or anecdote:** perhaps again to make a point, maybe something people know: *We all remember the moment when the ...,* or something they do not: *Last week in Singapore I got caught in the rain and...*

•)) **A fact:** preferably a striking one: or maybe challenging, provoking or surprising: *Research shows that if we give a customer cause to complain, they are likely to tell ten other people, but if we please them they will only tell one. Not a ratio to forget because...*

•)) **Drama:** something that surprises or shocks, or in some way delivers a punch: *The next ten minutes can change your life. It can ...*

•)) **A gesture:** something people watch and which gets their attention: *Some people in this company seem to think that money grows on trees* – said while tearing up a bank note and scattering the pieces

•)) **History:** this may be a general historical fact or one that evokes a common memory: *Five years ago, when we all knew we were at a turning point ...*

•)) **Curiosity:** an oddity, something that will surprise and have people waiting (perhaps eagerly) for the link with what is going to be said – it may be really odd or just out of context: *Now you may wonder why I should start with a reference to pachyderms; you may even wonder what it is.* (It is a thick-skinned quadruped; apparently irrelevant but ...)

•)) **Shock:** something totally unexpected, maybe seemingly inappropriate, that really makes people listen (though its relevance should be clear as you proceed): *Imagine this room full of dead bodies. It is a horrific thought, yet far more people than would fit in this room die every month from ...* (linked to something about charities, perhaps)

•)) **Silence:** this may seem a contradiction in terms: but can be used: *Please all remain absolutely quiet for a moment –* the speaker counts silently to ten and the gap begins to seem rather long – *that's how long it seems to customers waiting for Technical Support to answer the telephone; and it is too long*

•)) **A checklist:** this can spell out what is coming and there are certainly worse starts than: *There are four key issues I want to raise today. These are...*

Such devices are not mutually exclusive. They may be used in a variety of combinations and the above list is not exhaustive; you may well be able to think of more. Whatever you use, remember that the impact may come from several sentences rather than something as short as the examples used above. The first words, however, do need some careful thought and must be delivered in a way that achieves exactly the effect you are after.

Creating rapport

The creation of rapport is not subsidiary to gaining interest; the two must surely be inextricably bound up. So, think of anything you can build in that will foster group feeling, for example:

•)) Be careful of personal pronouns. There are moments to say you and others for we (and sometimes fewer for I). Thus, *We should consider...*, may well be better than, *You must ... or, I think you should ...*

•)) Use a (careful) compliment or two: *As experienced people you will ...*

•)) Use words that reinforce your position or competence (not to boast, but to imply you belong to the group): *Like you, I have to travel a great deal. I know the problems it makes with the continuity during an absence...*

•)) Be *enthusiastic*, but always genuinely so (this reminds me of the awful American expression that, *if you can fake the sincerity, then everything else is easy*; not so – back to enthusiasm). Real enthusiasm implies sincerity and both may be needed. Expressing enthusiasm tends to automatically make you more animated, so remember another old saying: *enthusiasm is the only good thing that is infectious.*

At the same time as the factors mentioned so far being important, there are also specific tasks to achieve in this first stage of the presentation. Again there may be a number of such tasks to consider. By way of example the following are often high on the list, to:

•)) Describe/define the topic

•)) State the objective

•)) Mention the planned duration of what you will do (not only do people like this, it also allows them to follow things better if they know when, for instance, the talk is about half-way through)

•)) Say why this is necessary

•)) Tell them something about the structure that you plan to use

•)) Say enough to catch their interest (not just for the moment, but in what is coming)

•)) Start, if necessary, to be seen to satisfy expectations

•)) Show why what you are doing is relevant – to *them*

•)) Encourage, if necessary, the audience to keep an open mind

•)) Reinforce (good) early first impressions (of yourself and the event).

The manner of delivery, emphasis and so on clearly also contribute to the effectiveness of this, indeed of every stage, and are therefore important to how you get your message across. But, perhaps most important of all, the beginning sets the scene for the audience. They begin to judge how it is going in their terms, so if they:

- •))) Feel it is beginning to be accurately directed at them

- •))) Feel their specific needs are being considered and respected

- •))) Feel the speaker is engaging

- •))) Begin to identify with what is being said – *that's right*.

then you will have them with you and can proceed to the main segment of the presentation – and can do so with confidence that a good reaction at the start can be a firm foundation for continuing success.

But the beginning is, by its nature, brief. It may be a few sentences or a few minutes. Certainly it should not unbalance the rest; you cannot spend twenty minutes leading up to two minutes and two points of main content! Whatever the kind of talk you give, it may be useful to note the percentage of the total duration that is effectively the beginning, and plan accordingly. Important though the beginning is, there is perhaps even more hanging on the next stage.

The middle – and the main message

This is the main part of the presentation and it is doubtless also the longest. During this stage there is the greatest need for clear organisation of the message and for clarity of purpose. Your key aims here should be to:

- •))) Put over the detail of the message

- •))) Maintain attention and interest

- •))) Do so clearly and in a manner appropriate to the audience.

Furthermore, if necessary, you may need to seek acceptance and, conversely, avoid people actively disagreeing with what you say. It is not always necessary to aim for agreement, but this is often an intention and may well be your prime objective, especially in a work context.

Given the length and greater complexity of the middle segment, it is important for it to be particularly well ordered. This includes the simple procedure of taking one point at a time. Here again I will try to practise what I preach, the following points will help this segment go well.

Putting over the main content

This needs:

- •)) *A logical sequence:* for example discussing a process in chronological order

- •)) *The use of what are effectively plenty of main and sub-headings:* this is, in part, what was referred to earlier as signposting, as: *There are three key points here: performance, method and cost. Let's take performance first …* It gives advance warning of what is coming and keeps the whole message from becoming rambling and difficult to follow because of it. Imagine what you say rather as a report looks: in written form the headings stand out in bold type – your headings – the divide between sections of what you say – should be clearly audible. The longer the duration of anything you do, the more important all this is

- •)) *Clarity:* people must understand what you say. There must be no verbosity. Not too much jargon. No convoluted arguments and no awkward turns of phrase. This is as much a question of words as of elements of greater length. Not only must there be no manual excavation devices, you must call a spade a spade and, should you actually speak of spades, they need to be relevant and interesting spades and fit logically in with your topic.

Note: never underestimate the need for care if you are to achieve prompt and clear understanding. Communications can be inherently difficult. You need to make sure that there is a considerable probability of a degree of definite cognition amongst those various different people in the audience, sorry, let me rephrase that. You need to be sure that everyone will easily understand what you say (Figure 6 spells out a useful mnemonic).

KISS

To help understanding:

Keep **I**t **S**imple, **S**peaker

or, as some put it less politely: Keep It Simple, Stupid.

So bear in mind such things as:

- Short words

- Short sentences

- Short paragraphs (sections)

- No more jargon than is appropriate

- Clarity of explanation

- Description that paints a picture

- Signpost intentions

- Group topics/points (groups of three to four work well; think how you remember a telephone number in short units).

Figure 6: *KISS*

Some examples here will help expand the point:

- •))) **Long words can sound pretentious:** so only say *sesquipedalian* rather than long word if there is a very good reason

- •))) **Certain phrases are not only convoluted, they can be annoying:** among a few that come to mind are: *at this moment in time* – when what is meant is *now*, or *in the not too distant future* – when *soon* would be better. Certainly you must avoid appearing to make things up – struggling to get something clear – as you go along: *Well, I suppose it's like … or rather, I mean …*

- •))) **The use of totally unnecessary words:** *basically* – at the start of a sentence, or unnecessary fashionable words like everything currently being *proactive* (what is wrong with active?) when for instance it might well be better just to talk about: *a response* rather than *a proactive response*

- •))) **Inadvertently giving a wrong impression:** either by being vague: does *quite nice* – applied, say, to a person mean they are good to know or is it merely being polite? Or by being imprecise: a *continuous process* might just be continual, for instance, depending on whether it is without interval or never ending. You can doubtless think of more, it is sometimes surprising how loosely language is used. In a formal situation you often do not receive much feedback or know that a false interpretation has been taken on board. You can therefore never think too carefully about exactly how you express things

- •))) **Be descriptive with language:** we might describe something as, *sort of shiny* or, to put over a specific feeling better as, *smooth as silk*. If it is the slipperiness of it that we want to emphasise then it may need more. I heard someone on the radio recently describe something as, *as slippery as a freshly buttered ice-rink*. No-one can possibly mistake that degree of slipperiness. Using similes (saying, *It is like …* as often as you can think of good allusions, always helps paint a picture). Examples are also important here. It is one thing to say, *This is a change that will be straightforward and cause no problems*, perhaps with the group thinking to themselves that if you expect them to believe that you will be selling them Tower Bridge next. It is quite another to say: *This is a change that will be straightforward and cause no problem* and then link it to something else: *It will be very like when the measurement system changed, there were plenty of fears about exactly what would happen, but the system and the training worked well. I don't think any of us would prefer to go back to the old ways now* – though, of course, the example must be appropriate (it would be no good in the example just given if the introduction of a new system in the past was regarded as being a disaster)

-))) **Be careful not to make wrong assumptions:** about people's level of knowledge, understanding, degree of past experience or existing views for instance, or what you say based on them will not hit home

-))) **Use visual aids:** a picture is worth a thousand words, they say, and checklists and exhibits – and more – are all a real help in getting the message across: let them speak for themselves (pause in speaking when you first show something – attention cannot be focused simultaneously on what you are saying and the visual) and make sure they *support* what you are doing rather than become the lead element – more of this in Chapter 6

-))) **Include gestures:** let your physical manner add emphasis, and inject appropriate feel and variety

-))) **Make your voice work:** in the sense that your tone makes it clear whether you are serious, excited, enthusiastic or any other emotion or emphasis you may wish to bring to bear in this way, as well as watching as it were the mechanics of the voice (speaking at the right volume and pace, for instance).

Note: a number of the above aspects, such as voice, which may appear to have been commented on only briefly here are returned to and expanded on in the next chapter.

So far so good, but there is more to be achieved than just putting over the content. You may well want people to agree with your ideas.

Gaining acceptance

This too can be assisted in a number of ways:

- •)) **Relating to the specific group:** general points and arguments may not be so readily accepted as those carefully tailored to the nature and experience of a specific audience (with some topics this is best interpreted as describing how things will affect *them* or what they will do for *them*)

- •)) **Provide proof:** certainly if you want to achieve acceptance, you need to offer something other than your word – as the speaker you may very well be seen as having a vested interest in your own ideas. Thus adding opinion, references or quoting test results from elsewhere and preferably from a respected and/or comparable source strengthens your case. This is evidenced by our experience in something like buying a car: are you most likely to believe the salesman who says, *This model will do more than fifty miles per gallon* or the one who says, *Tests done by the magazine* 'What Car?' *showed that this model does 52 miles per gallon?* Most of us will be more convinced by the latter.

It is particularly important not to forget *feedback* during this important stage:

- •)) **Watch:** for signs (nodding, fidgeting, yawning, whispered conversation, and just expressions) as to how your message is going down – try to scan the whole audience (you need in any case to maintain good eye contact around the group)

•))) **Listen:** too for signs – a restless audience, for example, actually has its own unmistakable sound

•))) **Ask:** for feedback. There are certainly many presentations where asking questions of the group is perfectly acceptable and it may be expected – even a brief show of hands may assist you

•))) **Aim:** to build in answers to any objections that you may feel will be in the mind of members of the audience, either mentioning the fact: *I know what you are thinking; it can't be done in the time. Well, I believe it can. Let me tell you how …* Or by not making a specific mention, but simply building in information intended to remove fears.

Even if you build in answers to likely disagreement, some issues may still surface, so you have always to be ready to expand your proof as you go.

When you have completed the main thrust of your message then you can move towards the end.

The end

Perhaps the first point to make here relates to a moment *before* the end. So be it, it is worth a mention. Good time-keeping is impressive. But it is not assumed. So flagging that the end is in sight may be useful, though you should allude reasonably specifically to what that means. If it is not just two more sentences, say so: *Right, I have two more points to make and then perhaps I may take a couple of minutes to summarise.* Or, *With five minutes of my time remaining, I would now like to …'*. Doing this is just signposting again, but if it engenders a feeling, which says something like: *My goodness, they look like finishing right on time,* then that can be good. Good time-keeping may be unexpected, but when it is in evidence it is always seen as a sign of professionalism.

Having said that, what are the requirements of a good ending? Two things predominate:

•)) A pulling together of the various points made

•)) Ending on a high note.

But first, consider some dangers.

The audience can notice an ending that goes less than just right in a disproportionate way, and, at worst, it can spoil the whole thing. So, beware of the following:

•)) **False endings:** there should be one ending (preferably flagged once); if you say, ... *and finally* ... three or four times then people understandably find it irritating

•)) **Wandering:** an end that never seems to actually arrive, though the nature of what is being said constantly makes it sound imminent

•)) **Second speech:** a digression, particularly a lengthy one, may be inappropriate close to the end when the audience are expecting everything to be promptly wrapped up

•)) **A rush to the finishing line:** this is a danger when time is pressing. It may be better to say you will overrun by a few minutes, or abbreviate some of your material earlier if time is running away from you, than to find yourself gabbling in the last few minutes as you race to reach the finish on time

•)) **Repetition:** or at least unnecessary repetition (for summary is another matter), is something else that can distract towards the close. Repetition: or at least unnecessary repetition ... enough. Point made.

With that in mind we turn to the positive. Summary is not the easiest thing to do succinctly and accurately. Hence if it is well done then it can be impressive. Consider this in another context, that of a written report. If, after reading twenty pages, you come to three paragraphs at the end that pull the whole thing neatly together and do so effectively, then you think better of the whole document (in addition, people who find summary difficult to execute respect those who do it well).

So, when you are speaking (or writing reports, for that matter) this is an element of the whole that is well worth careful preparation.

A pulling together or summary is a logical conclusion, it may link to the action you hope people will take following the presentation or simply present the final point. Whatever it contains, the ending should be comparatively brief. Having made the final point – with all the other factors now referred to continuing to be important throughout this stage – you need to end with something of a flourish.

That said, it is worth mentioning that your final words should never (or at least very rarely) be, *Thank you.* It is not that a thank you is not appropriate. Indeed, it may well be essential, but it does often make a poor last word. What happens is that the talk appears to tail away, a final punchy point being apt to be followed by something like: *Well perhaps I should end with a thank you, it has been a pleasure to be here. I appreciate you giving up some of your time for this ... so, many thanks to you all.* It is much better to have the thank you before the final point: *Thank you for being here, I am grateful for your attention. Now, a final word in conclusion...* This enables your final words to be more considered and punchy.

That final word may need to be based on some simple technique (rather like the opening, so only a few examples are given here):

- •)) **A question:** maybe repeating an opening question, maybe leaving something hanging in the air, maybe with the intention of prolonging the time people continue to think about the topic and what you have said

- •)) **A quotation:** particularly the sort that encapsulates a thought briefly

- •)) **A story:** allowing more time to put over, and emphasise, a concluding point

- •)) **An injunction to act:** where appropriate: *So, go out and...*

Having a clear link to what was said at the beginning works well. This may relate to content: *At the start I posed three questions, now let me see what the answers are ...* Or it may be just a phrase: *I used the words 'impossible task' at the start, but is what we are considering here an impossible task? I have tried to suggest otherwise ...* The neatness of such a technique seems to appeal. However you finish remember that your last remarks will linger in the mind a little more than much of what went before them. If you want to make people think, for instance, then your final words will act as a major part of what allows you to succeed in that aim.

Note: one point here that you need to bear in mind throughout the whole structure: as you put what you say together, remember that, while the beginning is important, the overall nature of what you say must remain good throughout the time you speak. It can sometimes be a trap to put good stuff first and then find that the quality tails away somewhat as you go on.

At the end of your talk, when you sit down, or later back in your office or home, perhaps with a large, well earned gin and tonic! (which incidentally is when you should have it; a drink before speaking 'to steady the nerves' is not recommended, and too much may loosen your inhibitions to the point where your tongue takes on a life of its own), what do you want? For the audience to:

- •)) Have had their expectations met (perhaps, better still surpassed)

- •)) Have understood everything that was said

- •)) Have followed the detail, logic and technicality of any argument you have been promoting

- •)) Warmed to you as a speaker (and felt whatever you may have wished to project, for example, trust or belief in your expertise, was projected)

- •)) Seen what was done and how it was done as appropriate to them.

You might want to add to this list, wanting people to have found the whole thing interesting, stimulating, whatever … any adjectives you choose need to reflect your circumstances and intention.

You may not feel, at this stage, that you will ever look forward to speaking formally on your feet. But you are certainly likely to find that you can fairly quickly come to enjoy the feeling of having made one that has gone as you wished, and find that one that has gone really well produces real satisfaction for both the audience and the speaker. And, who knows, if you follow all the advice here you may even begin to find that as well as becoming more certain of the process and, as a result, doing a better job on it, you do begin to draw some real pleasure from it.

The principles reviewed in this chapter, and the thread of the way a clear structure is used, constitute a major part of all the influences that can make your speaking effective. But there is more to it than that. A variety of tricks of the trade can also help to augment what you do, maximise its impact and increase the certainty of it meeting your objectives precisely. It is to these that we turn in the next chapter.

CHAPTER 5

Tricks of the Trade

A speaker who does not strike oil in ten minutes should stop boring.

Louis Nizer

Though it may provide a place for it, structure cannot inject a sparkle. Having dealt with the overall structure of a talk or presentation in the last chapter, which one might sensibly regard as the equivalent of solid foundations to a building, here we turn to how manner and behaviour can inject additional meaning, emphasis and feeling into how you speak and thus how you come over. The factors mentioned here necessarily form a varied list as the process is dissected. No apology for that, it is the nature of the subject. Further it should be clear at the outset that the factors discussed are not mutually exclusive. One of the complexities of this whole overall process is that there is a good deal happening at one and the same time. This means that there is much to think about, indeed orchestrate, at the same time. A clear understanding of the processes involved and the development of the right reflexes and habits are thus important to an ability to orchestrate the whole, and to fine-tuning your presentations as they move along.

Everything that follows is important because people do a lot more than just listen. They *experience* what you do. Everything about the manner and demeanour of the speaker contributes to the overall feeling people take away. And, in this, non verbal factors are as important as verbal ones. Think how a smile changes your view of someone. So, incidentally, smiling is something you may need to do consciously. How you look has already been mentioned; here we start, not with appearance but with how you look.

Using your eyes

Eye contact with the members of the group makes an important contribution to the overall way in which a speaker is perceived. Here we review how you can maximise the impact you make in this respect. Consider first what constitutes good eye contact. Overall two factors are particularly important, it should be:

- •)) Comprehensive, taking in all of the group (or all parts of a large audience) and continuing throughout the presentation

- •)) Deliberate and noticeable (this means that eye contact must be maintained for longer than would be normal in ordinary conversation – perhaps for periods of four to five seconds rather than two to three).

Thus it is very much something that can only become truly effective once it becomes a habit, and it is a habit that you must work to acquire. To digress for a moment: everything of this sort may seem a little daunting initially. If you can remember learning to drive, then the same thing probably applied with that. To begin with certain aspects of the process seemed virtually physically impossible, but soon, almost without you realising it, they became habits and the whole process came together. Thus something such as checking your rear view mirror at certain points as you drive becomes all but automatic. In presenting there are numbers of things that will acquire similar characteristics and eye contact is certainly one of them. Initially, however, you need to work at it becoming more automatic, and later at responding to it when appropriate. After all there is no point in scanning the group if you learn nothing from it, and if it appears too automatic then it will have a less positive effect on the group, who after all want to feel you are really interested in them.

On the other hand, consider what *bad* eye contact – looking too long at your notes, away from the group (into the corner of the room or out of the window – *What's so fascinating?* people will ask themselves), or at one or two favoured members of the group to the exclusion of the others – can lead to. It can mean you create little or no rapport with the audience. It can mean:

- •)) You appear anxious, nervous or, at worst, incompetent

- •)) You seem to lack sincerity

- •)) You lose the level of credibility you seek

- •)) You obtain little or no feedback

- •)) The presentation may seem to falter (especially because of any lack of feedback)

- •)) There is no opportunity for feedback to lead to certain kinds of fine-tuning as the talk proceeds. For example: feedback might indicate incomprehension of some point, which can then be elaborated (something to watch for particularly with technical points and figures).

Contrast this with *good* eye contact – which shows the speaker is in touch with the audience. It can give an impression, which produces a number of benefits:

- •)) It establishes rapport with the group, which demonstrates you care about them and increases their belief that the presentation will be right for them

- •)) This interest in the group increases credibility, trust and attention

- •)) The speaker appears more confident, more assertive, more professional, more expert (it can enhance any intended feeling of this sort)

- •)) It allows feedback (it is useful to know if people appear attentive, interested, supportive or bored or indifferent)

- •)) Such feedback can be used to fine-tune the detail of what you are doing

- •)) All positive benefits felt by the speaker act in some way to build confidence and this, in turn, helps improve the way in which you come over.

For example, a speaker trying to put over something difficult or contentious will find their manner (and perhaps use of feedback) contributes much to achieving their aims, or vice versa.

Watch here for, and avoid, any automatic pattern developing. It is disconcerting for an audience to see a speaker going through a routine of looking at each section of the group in, say, a regular clockwise circuit. Remember that good, natural-looking eye contact is a habit to foster (and you will not develop exactly what you want perfectly or instantly). Remember too that if you are:

- •)) Well prepared

- •)) Familiar with your material

- •)) Working from clear notes (that do not need lengthy attention to spot what comes next)

- •)) Comfortable in your environment

- •)) Relaxed and confident

then your ability to produce good eye contact is enhanced.

Try it

It may be useful to conduct a short exercise with yourself to demonstrate and develop this technique. Speak for a minute or two in front of a mirror, *without speaking out loud or worrying about exactly what is being said* (though you can follow a planned preparation in your mind and with notes in front of you if necessary). This allows greater concentration to go on what the eyes should be doing and greater emphasis can be given to this aspect. Watch your face and see how your eyes are moving.

Concentration on any one factor amongst many, isolating it for attention will always help you fine-tune exactly how a particular aspect of the process is being utilised.

Next we consider the most obvious speaker's resource: the voice.

Using your voice

The first step towards maximising what can be done with the voice is to be relaxed and project it effectively, something we touched on in reviewing how to overcome nerves. The voice has an almost infinite capacity to vary meaning and emphasis. Just how something is expressed can add a great deal to its impact. Often even tiny changes in tone can vary meaning. Consider a simple sentence with the emphasis placed on particular words:

•)) It is your *voice* that makes the difference

•)) It is *your* voice that makes the difference.

Consider too the slight difference that puts a question mark at the end of a sentence:

•)) You are not sure

•)) You are not sure?

Now consider these two factors together:

•)) You are *not* sure?

So the voice needs to be used in two key ways. It must be clearly audible, and it must have variety – varying pace and pitch – to produce a suitable emphasis, and simply sound interesting. A dull monotone will spark no interest and prevent there being an emphasis on anything. Here we review the way in which this occurs and consider ways of achieving what you want from your voice.

It is always something of a shock to the system for people to hear their own voices, as when you record something and play it back (on video in training sessions it may be seen and heard). Your voice is perhaps a particular shock, no-one ever hears themselves as others hear them unless they are recorded. However, some faults, such as talking too fast (often an effect of nerves), can be quickly corrected once people have heard how they really sound.

Try it

Try recording a minute or two of your voice as a test. If you have not heard yourself recently it may be a shock, but recent exposure to how you *actually* sound is certainly useful if you feel you want to make any changes to the way you come over.

Two further points about the voice are important: audibility and emphasis.

Audibility

For the less experienced speaker, judging whether you will be heard clearly at the back of the room is a worry, but audibility is in fact largely only a matter of speaking somewhat louder than is usual in conversation. The simplest rule is to *direct what you say at the most distant part of the room* (keep the people in the back row in mind). It is important to get this right – a test was suggested earlier – clearly if people cannot actually hear you this is the ultimate problem. Though there is a story told of a speaker pausing to say, *Can you hear me okay at the back of the room?* They are answered by a voice saying, *Yes, but I'm prepared to swap with someone who can't.* Even a situation in which people are hearing only with a struggle is also dangerous, and it will change the audience's view of you. The results of this may include the following:

- •)) The audience tends to become irritated

- •)) Audience attention is less on the message than on struggling to hear

- •)) The speaker may well be regarded as nervous, inconsiderate, inexpert or worse

•)) A low voice tends also to be monotonous and thus boring.

On the other hand, a good clear delivery has advantages that are the antithesis of the above; it gives a positive impression of the speaker as someone competent and commanding attention.

In addition, speaking up tends to be one factor that helps you inject more animation and enthusiasm into a presentation. It encourages you to use gestures and generally affects the professional way in which you come over.

Emphasis

The use of the voice to inject emphasis and animation to what you do is vital. A presentation that is put over in a lively and animated tone of voice, that *sounds* interesting and which varies its pace and pitch, will always go over better than one that is delivered on some kind of monotone.

Here we review a number of seemingly simple issues that contribute to making up the total impression of your message and *how* it goes over. We start with the reverse of voice: no voice at all.

That is a ...

... pause.

What is *not* said is just as important as what is said. The pause can do a number of things:

•)) Allow what has just been said to sink in

•)) Give time for the audience to interpret or analyse what has been said (for example, in the way that a rhetorical question can prompt thought)

•)) Focus attention on something other than what is said (as when using a visual aid)

•)) Add drama (hence the so-called 'dramatic pause')

•)) Punctuate (making a real break to separate one point from another).

There is another benefit of the pause, one that helps you – it *gives you time to think*. This is especially important as a common fault is to speak too fast. Doing so makes it all the more difficult to think as you go and prevents you from exercising the necessary fine-tuning as you progress. Regular pauses are thus important, even if they are no more than punctuation and a chance to draw breath and think.

There is, however, a real difficulty with pauses – everyone thinks that they may overdo it and that the pause will then turn into an embarrassment. This is a feeling that the instigator of a pause feels much more deeply than others, and that a formal speaker feels more acutely than members of the group addressed.

Try it

You can demonstrate this to yourself very simply: ask someone to help you with a short experiment, simply ask them to listen to you as you speak and then, at a convenient point, pause and count to ten slowly to yourself. Then continue for a few moments more. When you stop, ask them what they think was the duration of the pause. It is likely to seem longer to you; indeed your just counting ten slowly may seem to you to take an age. Time is relative.

Also practise saying a sentence that you know needs a pause to be made within it. Say it several times and vary the length of the pause to change how it will sound and the effect it will have on the listener. A tape recorder will make this and other exercises that much more revealing and useful.

If you need to pause and are worried about it becoming too long, or know you cannot judge the length you want, the solution is simple. You literally count silently to yourself (do not worry, no-one will know!). In so doing you can take advantage of the fact that a pause can do a number of the things mentioned above and add something to your presentation. It is, not least, a part of overall pace, it adds variety and acts to slow any tendency for your tongue to rush away from you. Because of its importance you may find it useful to have a prompt in your notes to show where you plan to take any significant pause. This could be simply in the form of a – – – - **bold** (or coloured) dotted line.

The pause is a valuable device and wisely used can enhance any speech. Remember it was only the pause in, *The name is Bond ... James Bond* that made it a catch phrase. And I would bet every new actor coming to the part over the years has practised that pause!

Next, let us return to what you do say.

Use words wisely

You cannot speak without using words, but what is important here is how your exact choice of words can make a real – distinct – great – considerable – powerful – pronounced – significant difference to the totality of the message that you put over. This is sufficiently important to make having a thesaurus to hand during preparation very useful. A poor choice of words is easy to make, perhaps compounded by any nerves you may be experiencing, and this is a common cause of presentations not being as effective as they might be. It can even be that one wrong word can switch an audience off or confuse them to a significant degree. For example, I once heard a business presentation made: the presenter began by describing the organisation for which they worked. He said it was *a fragmented organisation*. It transpired that there was a positive point here, he meant to describe the way the organisation was arranged as a series of different divisions reflecting an accurate interface with their customers. But fragmented (literally a fragment is a part broken off a whole) was the wrong word, it sounded negative and his audience looked puzzled. Literally in the first minute of his talk this was enough to seriously dilute the positive effect he intended.

Sometimes the problem here is less one of incorrect thinking, and thus selection, than of not thinking at all. In other words, the first word that comes to mind may well not be the best for the circumstances. The audience must be a major factor in your selection, dictating, for example, what degree of technicality may be appropriate, as well as a straightforward level and style of language. The danger of too much jargon has already been mentioned, but is a sufficient hazard to deserve repeating.

Consider the difference one word can make to meaning and emphasis, for instance in the sentence that follows:

The choice of words makes a *real* difference to the effect they have on a group.

Try it

Take a number of sentences, perhaps from a presentation you have made or must make, and try substituting alternative words to seek more precise meaning. If you take a bland word to start with it will lead you most easily into the process. To set you off try replacing the bland word *big* in the following:

Improving my presentation skills could make a *big* difference in my job.

What word might imply a difference in your ability to do something useful or important and do it effectively? – *significant* or *practical* perhaps?

Try again, picking your own sentences.

As was suggested earlier, consider how the sentence 'The choice of words makes a big difference to the effect they have on a group' can vary if one of the following words replaced *big: distinct; great; considerable; powerful; pronounced*. Which sounds strongest? Think of the different contexts in which you would want different meanings for this: *powerful* to suggest that what is said carries influence, *pronounced* perhaps when the need is greater technical accuracy or precision.

You can apply exactly the same sort of thinking to phrases. For example, continuing the example above: 'Improving my presentation skills *will make me better able to tackle important parts of my job*' has a much more specific meaning than: 'Improving my presentations skill *will be very helpful*'. And if what that will do is make you better able to get across your ideas and influence events for the better, then why not say that?

Try it

This procedure can be repeated again focusing on:

- Bland words or phrases (big, very, nice)
- Clichés, and meaningless words or phrases (*due to the fact that* – when you mean: *because*)
- Superfluous elements (sentences that begin *Basically*, ... for no good reason)
- Words and sentences.

Experimenting with the differences you can make, and your ability to find words and phrases that match the precise nuance you want, will certainly lead to a more expressive style.

Incidentally, picking up a point in the boxed paragraph, why is it that so many of us say things like the ubiquitous yet superfluous word *basically* that peppers many a speech? For the most part it is a form of pause or punctuation that becomes a habit. The same is true of the ubiquitous ums and errs. Rather than concentrating in horror at their incidence, something that will likely increase them, concentrate on a more precise form of words and good punctuation and they will decline with your hardly thinking about it.

Word choice can be affected by what one might call 'word-fashion'. We hear words entering the language or being used in new ways all the time – language and language use is nothing if not dynamic. But words have a life cycle. Use them too early and they are misunderstood or annoy. I still twitch when BBC radio uses the Americanism of *upcoming events*; the more traditional *forthcoming* will suit me a while longer. Use words too late in their life cycle and they are overworked and have lost their power, and may annoy. Surely a classic example of this is the description *user friendly*. Once upon a time it was a neat, new and descriptive phrase; now every gadget in the visible universe is automatically described as user friendly; it has lost all power. I once asked someone in the computer world about the phrase and was told: *User friendly means something is very complicated, but not as complicated as next year's model* – sorry, I digress. Words do change and some eventually fall out of use, so if you use such words it may sound odd and is best avoided. For instance, while some people still listen to the wireless, most now tune in to the radio.

Note: a small, but significant point that is worth noting is that a good many abbreviations do not sound right verbally. So avoid saying things like etc. – it may be used in print, but lacks any elegance when spoken.

How you put it

As well as choosing the right words and phrases, the way in which something is said makes a difference to how it goes across. This is true in a general sense: variety, pace and so on, but this also involves various specific techniques that can add to the power of what is said. For example:

•)) **Repetition:** Repeating a well chosen word or phrase can add emphasis. For some reason three times seems to work best. Who does not know Winston Churchill's famous speech containing the words: *We will fight them on the beaches*? The 'we will fight them' phrase repeats to particularly good effect. This can work well in more mundane circumstances. You can repeat a phrase to focus on the sense of it, you can repeat a phrase to make what is said more memorable, and you can repeat a phrase in a way that builds the confidence that comes across as you speak. Just as the last sentence does. This is not something to overuse, but it is something to consider and use regularly

•)) **Go quiet:** you can add power in various ways, but dropping the voice is sometimes seen as a risk and underused. This works best at the end of a point – 'We must find ways of cutting costs. Our very survival depends on it, and if we do (drops voice) *we can emerge from this period much stronger*'. The final phrase said slowly and softly commands attention and makes a strong point. It also seems less usual than giving a heavy emphasis and perhaps gains from that too

•)) **Complexity/clarity relationship:** here a final point is thrown into sharp relief by a longer than expected run up to it – *Time is not on our side, it is already October and the year will soon be over, what must be done before Christmas is already daunting, <u>but we can do this</u>. Let me explain why I am sure of that.* The words that are underlined in the last sentence, said more slowly than the run in, and with some emphasis, can be made to make a strong point

•)) **Wrong:** avoid words or phrases that someone in the audience will twitch at because they are ungrammatical or wrong in some way. So do not say: *very unique, about 10.345%*, or talk about *future planning* (you can plan the past? This is tautology).

The idea here is that a manner that might be too much 'over the top' in normal conversation can work well in a more formal situation when you are on your feet. Perhaps the way to think about this is that you can usefully exaggerate the devices of everyday speech when you are making a presentation. Just as the dramatic pause needs to be sufficiently long to show itself for what it is, so the way you speak needs to be tailored to ensure it produces the emphasis you want. This is an area to think about, experiment with and find styles that you are comfortable with and which do the job you want.

Ultimately you have to select not simply the right word or phrase, but a well selected flow of words that continue throughout the presentation. Perhaps more important than anything is clarity of meaning, linked perhaps with description which is pleasing as well as useful in conjuring up a picture. The next section provides an additional digression to exemplify this key aspect of putting the message across.

Getting to the nub of the message

Your job when speaking is to actively select a method of delivery that allows your true meaning and description to shine through, making it easy, noticeably easy, for the audience to understand. Psychologists use the phrase cognitive cost to refer to the effort needed by the recipient of a communication to work out what it means. People like there to be a low cognitive cost, something coming over easily, and they hate a high one. They especially like it when they expect, for whatever reason, something to be complex and difficult to work out and it is then – perhaps unexpectedly – made easy. The speaker who makes it easy for their audience to understand is always appreciated for that fact, if nothing else.

Business communication often springs from habits and style that obscure the meaning.

The much quoted 'standard progress report' (reproduced as I once saw it on an office wall) is a spoof of the kind of writing that is all too common in business circles.

Standard progress report

For Those with No Progress to report

During the survey period, which ended on 14 February, considerable progress has been made in the preliminary work directed towards the establishment of the initial activities. [*We are getting ready to start, but have not done anything yet.*] The background information has been surveyed and the functional structure of the component parts of the cognisant organisation has been clarified. [*We have looked at the project and decided that George would lead it.*]

Considerable difficulty has been encountered in the selection of optimum approaches and methods but this problem is being attacked vigorously and we expect the development phase to proceed at a satisfactory rate [*George is looking through the handbook*]. In order to prevent unnecessary duplication of previous efforts in the same field, it was necessary to establish a survey team, which has conducted a rather extensive tour through various departments with immediate access to the system [*George and Harry had a nice time visiting everyone*].

The Steering Committee held its regular meeting and considered rather important policy matters pertaining to the overall organisational levels of the line and staff responsibilities that devolve on the personnel associated with the specific assignments resulting from the broad functional specifications [*untranslatable – sorry*]. It is believed that the rate of progress will continue to accelerate as necessary personnel are made available for the necessary discussions [*We will get some work done as soon as we find somebody who knows something*].

In speaking, the same tendency can occur. In the example that follows, an initial statement is gradually simplified until clarity appears, as it were out of the mist. The final version is, I think, a good turn of phrase, but it is not definitive; the infinite potential of language means that many versions are possible. They will not all, of course, be similarly clear. Such a chain of improvement could doubtless continue and has in any case ultimately to reflect and suit the individual style of the speaker and the nature of the audience. You would want to say this sentence a little differently; and would feel your version was best.

Er ....Um ... I suppose what I mean basically is what we intrinsically desire to, well, put over is sometimes not what is communicated on account of the ....er.... message being sort of implanted – inserted that is – in a disorganisation of expression not cognisant with real – that is complete – comprehension.

Awful: too hesitant, too complex in words, too laborious of expression, disorganised and too long = unclear.

What we intrinsically want to put over is sometimes not what is communicated, on account of the messages being implemented in a disorganisation of expression not cognisant with comprehension.

Better. The meaning is beginning to be clear, but 'businesspeak' still predominates and the wording is still laborious, overcomplicated and lacking in description = unclear.

What we really want to say is sometimes not really clear because the true message is hidden amongst too much that is superfluous and cannot therefore be transferred to the audience.

Better still. The meaning is surely clear but it is still awkward and lacking in description = think again.

> Sometimes the clarity we seek to convey is obscured, hidden like a diamond amongst broken ice. If so, and audience cannot appreciate the intended meaning of the message.
>
> *Right. I think it is clear. I like the way it sounds (though next time I might well put it differently and feel it was improved). It is also the most succinct.*

Note: in passing, another comment may be made here regarding punctuation. The *er* and *um* and *sort of* in the first part of the example act as punctuation. The next versions are lengthy and might be considered to need more punctuation. The last is simply stated and punctuated and as a result can be spoken fluently. *A good speaker is conscious of the punctuation inherent in what is delivered, and this makes for a good pace and correct emphasis as well as assisting to achieve understanding.*

The words and phrases you use must be well chosen, but they do not, on their own, do the complete job.

The sound of ...

How words are said is just as important as what they are. A variety of factors – the pitch of the voice, articulation, inflection, and the emphasis given to particular words or phrases (or sentences for that matter), are all instrumental in achicving your exact intended meaning. These matters are worth a separate word each:

- •)) **Pitch:** this is the note – higher or lower – of your voice. Extremes away from the norm may add emphasis, and, of course, be coupled with other factors: for example saying something slower and lower can add a note of gravitas. This is particularly important where you want to give the impression of such factors as importance, impatience, excitement or interest. Imagine the way the strength of a negative is affected by the pitch, if it sounds too light it may be taken to mean 'maybe', yet it can also be said in a way that unmistakably means NO or **NO**!

•))) **Articulation:** this is the clarity of sound you put into what you say. If you mumble something that is compounded by going at too fast a pace, you will not be understood. Even if you are understood, it is a strain for the listeners. They will not like it and may miss things as they struggle to keep up. Some things need particular clarity, for example:

•))) Figures (you may not want 15% mistaken for 50%)

•))) The sound of Fs and Ss

•))) The sound at the end of words.

Before anything else, your meaning must be clear. This may well seem obvious, but still you may benefit from double-checking your clarity using a tape recorder: see Figure 7: *Getting your tongue round it.*

If you sto dumble (sic), then try not to flap. We all do it and audiences understand. Take a moment, perhaps make an aside as well as pause – *let me put my teeth back in* – and say again whatever made you stumble and was unclear. At the end of your talk it is likely that no-one will even remember such a fault – provided that such do not occur every few sentences throughout the time you speak.

•))) **Inflection:** this is the way differing sound and adding an additional meaning to a phrase (in the way that there may be a clear sound that implies that a question mark follows a word – this can be important, for example a rhetorical question must be clearly recognisable as such to have its effect). This links closely to the next item below.

•))) **Emphasis:** this might be described as the verbal equivalent of **bold** or *italic* type.

Now, before we continue, take a moment to consider the details of the following mathematical problem: a man and woman live 10 miles apart. It is their habit in the summer to meet at a pub located between their homes. The man walks at 6 mph and the woman, who has shorter legs, at 4 mph. Now the man has a dog – a prize greyhound

Even assuming you do not speak too quickly, it is a common fault to speak less than clearly. In a presentation, while you must speak naturally, you need to exaggerate the articulation to produce clarity and allow expression, which can never come over as well as you want if you are simply indistinct.

You may find it useful to practise intentionally awkward phrases (in private by all means). Try repeating some of the following traditional tongue-twisters and sentences containing similar sounding words:

- Red leather, yellow leather
- She says she shall sew a sheet
- She sells seashells by the seashore
- We're your well-wishers

Also, my favourite:
I'm not a pheasant plucker, I'm a pheasant plucker's son, and I'll go on plucking pheasants till the pheasant plucking's done.

And:
- His story is now history
- The Leith police dismisseth us
- Get some nice ice, not some nice mice
- He hears his hiss

You may have others you know and can try. Some combinations are so apt to tie the tongue they are best avoided, and this too is something it is useful to watch out for in preparation.

FIGURE 7: *Getting your tongue round it*

and he has cleverly trained it to run between them as they walk – the dog chases to and fro, to and fro all the time they walk to meet and gets a great deal of exercise. The dog runs at 9 mph. How far does it run, before the two meet at the pub?

This may seem confusing. It is flagged as being mathematical (that alone is sufficient to ensure some people will give up on it!). There is much talk about people, pubs, summer walks and the dog running to and fro to get its exercise. None of these details matter. Work it out: the man and woman are closing the distance between them at 10 mph (6 + 4, with me so far?) so it takes them an hour to meet – 10 miles at 10 mph. How far does the dog run? In an hour at 9 miles per hour? See – you are a mathematician! The point is that the key facts that make the calculation easy to do are buried, they appear – without emphasis – amongst a lot of irrelevant detail.

Emphasis is always important. It is especially important in two ways to:

•)) Ensure that the main points shine through, and that differing elements of a presentation (main points, examples, asides and explanation, say) are clear and stand out from the whole (just as different sorts of type face look different on a well set out page of print)

•)) Inject animation and make what is said more interesting.

Try it

You can demonstrate the power of emphasis to yourself very easily, and experiment with it. For example, select a word or phrase the meaning of which can be changed just by saying it with a different emphasis. If you take one simple word: No. It can be said in a way that is:

- definite

- very definite

- clearly is undecided

- might mean maybe

You can, I am sure, think of more.

With a phrase it may be where the emphasis is put that makes the difference:

- '*I* am quite sure'

- 'I *am* quite sure'

- 'I am quite *sure*'.

Select a few and practise (again try using a tape recorder if you really want to hear the difference you can create).

With emphasis goes *power*. Think of the movie villains. They do not all shout, some of the most menacing are softly spoken – it shows how many different ways there are of achieving what you want.

All these different factors must be orchestrated together. This may sound complex, but again the initial task is to develop some good habits and, above all, to remain conscious of the possibilities. The way you use your voice can potentially add so much to the way you present.

Next consider something at the other end of the body from where the voice emanates.

Footwork

Superficially the feet may seem to have little to do with presentation. Not so. Feet, and the stance that goes with them, are both important elements in the way a speaker both feels and thus comes over. Here therefore are some guidelines to help ensure comfort and assist in making a good impression. Note that footwork takes us into total posture and movement; other aspects of this are dealt with under the next heading (*Arms and hands*).

Though it may be true that people in the audience rarely look at a presenter's feet (but you may still need to make sure your shoes are clean), if you make mistakes in the way you stand they will notice both the feet and the results. The first question to be investigated is therefore 'to move or not to move'. The extremes can both cause problems:

First, *too much movement*, this:

- •)) Can make the speaker appear nervous

- •)) May channel energy away from more important areas

- •)) May become a distraction, in itself

- •)) Could put you in the wrong place at the wrong time (out of reach of the projector or your notes).

Secondly, *too little movement*:

- •)) Can look uncomfortable

- •)) Can actually be uncomfortable (you easily get stiff)

- •)) Restricts the use of gestures and makes for a static approach.

Circumstances affect cases. You cannot move so much standing behind a lectern as you can working from behind a table or in the open, for instance. Always you need to find an 'ideal' amount of foot movement that will suit you and seem appropriate to the audience. As examples of the principle, such an ideal might include how you:

- •)) Stand up straight (slouching looks slovenly – the best way of avoiding this is to imagine a string attached to the middle of the top of the head pulling straight upwards)

- •)) Keep your feet just a little apart (shoulder width – to maintain an easy balance)

- •)) Always move just a little to avoid cramp and add some variety

- •)) Move purposively (making it clear, for example, that you are moving to be near equipment or to address a questioner more directly).

Overall a relaxed, comfortable and yet professional stance will communicate confidence (perhaps even beyond the level that is felt). The most suitable stance may vary depending on both the nature and duration of the event. For example, some meetings are more formal than others, some are more participative (a speaker may need to walk into the open space of a U-shaped conference layout to address people more individually), and some are simply longer (a trainer working with a group all day might acceptably lean back, effectively half sitting against the table at the front, whereas a fifteen-minute presentation from a lectern may need greater formality and allow less variety).

Stance can make a point too: I once saw a speaker sit cross-legged on top of a table and start his speech by saying, *Not all accountants are boring.*

It is even worth mentioning choice of shoes. I find lengthy lecturing gets very uncomfortable in leather-soled shoes and prefer the modern style with soft, air enhanced soles; these are available in formal styles if necessary. I presume that having to walk up several unfamiliar steps to a lectern and stand for a while with electric wires for projectors and lights around your feet, is a hazard for women in some styles of high heeled shoes and similar thought is perhaps necessary there. But on this I would not presume to say more.

Try it

It is practically impossible to try out stances in isolation – have a go if you like – without becoming self-conscious and stilted. But do think positively about the practicalities of this as you face individual presentational situations, and do not run before you can walk. By which I mean you may, for instance, create considerable rapport and emphasis by walking into the centre of a U-shaped meeting layout to deal with or make a particular point, but this will fall flat if you have to race back to your notes in mid-sentence and in panic to see what should come next.

So, with feet firmly on the floor we can turn to the other aspects that make up the totality of stance and posture.

Arms and hands

Both arms and hands are very much more visible and noticeable to the audience than feet, what is more they give rise to one of the most asked questions from presenters: *What do I do with my hands?* Awkwardness about what to do with them can be a distraction to the speaker. And if they are awkward then they become a distraction to the audience. They should be an asset to the speaker and make a positive impression on the members of the audience. They will serve in this way if gestures made are appropriate and then naturally executed. Some immediate examples of use and effect will help illustrate their importance:

- •)) Too static a pose is awkward and distracting (and may look too formal or imply nerves)

- •)) Some static positions look protective (implying fear of the audience). This is true of standing with arms folded or clasped in front of the body

•⟩⟩ Too much arm waving seems nervous and is equated with fidgeting (this is especially so of arm waving and hand gestures that do not seem to relate to what is being said – the Magnus Pyke school of presentation).

Conversely:

•⟩⟩ A comfortable 'resting' position for hands and arms is comfortable for speaker and audience alike

•⟩⟩ Appropriate gestures and animation add interest, enthusiasm and emphasis. They give an impression of confidence and thus expertise.

Two key elements here are worth an individual word.

Resting

The most obvious natural position is simply standing with both hands hanging loosely by the sides. The problem here is that many people find that the more they think about it the harder it is to be natural. The only route is thus to think about it first, to decide on a number of positions that can be adopted as bases from which a period of greater animation can commence; then forget about it. Remember that, for men, in a business suit, one hand in a trouser pocket may have an appropriate appearance; two never does, it just looks slovenly. One useful alternative to arms by the sides is to give your hands something specific and appropriate to *do*, for example:

•⟩⟩ Hold some suitable item (perhaps a pen)

•⟩⟩ Hold onto something (perhaps a corner of a lectern) – one hand is best here, using two can make it look as if you are hanging on for protection, so, even with one hand, avoid white knuckles!

This is certainly an area that can benefit from some thought; however, what works best is a fluid transition between these things. A natural pose, then shifting to another, then making a gesture and moving back again works well. Rest assured it comes with practice and try to avoid becoming hyper-conscious of it. If you relax and forget about it you will adopt a natural pose and manner, one which will look right.

Gestures

These should not be overdone, but should be useful and relate to the words being used. Above all there must be some. To use no animation at all always gives a lacklustre impression. What can you do? Here are some examples:

- •)) A simple directional pointing – to a slide, a member of the group, or more intangibly (a point into space as you say something about, *the world at large*)

- •)) A fist banged on the table – *'NO!'*

- •)) A width gesture (like the fisherman's 'one that got away' gesture) to indicate size – *Enormous potential*

- •)) Counting on the fingers – *First, we need … secondly …* (though as was said earlier, be careful not to lose count! – people notice)

- •)) Holding up and showing an item – *This xxxx will …*

- •)) A dramatic gesture – throwing something (carefully!).

You can no doubt think of more and must search for ones that you find comfortable to use, that will become a natural part of your approach. It is an idea, at least until confidence builds, to use a mark in your notes to prompt you to make key gestures.

Here again we are seeing something that is dependent, at least in part, on acquiring habits. Do not worry about it too much and it will become natural, though knowing what you are aiming at will help.

Try it

This can be another area where practice in isolation may be so artificial as to help little. Two things are worthwhile:

- Make a point of demonstrating to yourself just how much of a message comes over via the gestures. Next time you watch something on the television where someone is making a speech, turn the sound down and watch the visual alone. A few moments even will make the point.

- Actively build in certain key gestures, as was suggested with a prompt in your notes, so that you do not fail to include them, but do not worry too much about what happens in between. You will find with practice that you begin to link them up and a more fluid pattern is built into your overall manner.

At this point we turn to something rather different. You might imagine that you are in full flow, using all the principles of structure and delivery so far discussed. Everything is going really well, to your surprise your nerves have retreated into the background and then, suddenly ... *crash, someone who has crept into the back of the meeting room with a tray of cups drops the lot. All heads turn ...*

Unexpected accidents

With the best will in the world (even assuming adequate preparation) not everything is going to go right every time. Sometimes there will be unexpected accidents and these can:

- •)) Throw the speaker off their stride

- •)) Disrupt the attention of the audience.

They may, of course, do both, bearing in mind that it is mostly fear of the second that causes people to allow the first to occur. You may not know exactly what is going to happen, but you can consider in advance how to best deal with the unexpected.

First adopt the right attitude:

- •)) Accept that accidents do, occasionally, happen

- •)) Accept that they do disrupt attention and cannot be ignored

- •)) Remember that forewarned is forearmed.

All sorts of things can happen, elsewhere in the room as mentioned above, or it may be you who causes the accident. You spill a jug of water or put up the next slide and it is not the next slide. Reactions can vary and include reduced credibility, laughter, distraction, even pity. What is needed is a systematic response, a mode of dealing with things that you drop into almost automatically, matching the specifics of what you do to the circumstances of the moment. The following provide such a basis for action:

- •)) **Acknowledge it:** (it is no good pretending nothing has happened). This can range from saying, *Oh, dear* to saying something more humorous: *Don't expect me to pay for that!* if something is broken, for example. Not least, this gives you a moment to think what to do next

- •)) **Consider the options:** which may range from a further remark or two while you sort something out, to taking an impromptu break while the situation is recovered

- •)) **Take the chosen action:** quickly and quietly and calmly (remember the old saying: more haste less speed)

- •)) **Communicate:** simply tell people what is happening (this may take no longer than the action itself)

- •)) **Restart:** with some punch, rather as if starting a new point.

Remember that the audience are on your side when disaster strikes. The most usual thought to flash through the minds of members of the group is: *Thank goodness it isn't me having to deal with that!* So if something happens that could not have been avoided, then a smooth recovery is itself impressive and builds the perception of competence you no doubt want to project.

Certain things can be planned for pretty specifically. For example, if you use an overhead projector – there are many organisations that have one these days despite PowerPoint taking over the world – what happens if the bulb blows? Does the machine have a facility simply to switch over to a second bulb? If so, then a simple acknowledgement of what you are doing and flicking a switch sorts the problem. If not, can you carry on without the projector (or is an impromptu break while the bulb is changed possible)? The answer may depend on the nature and location of the presentation, but having a few options in mind will make it easier to cope with.

Something else you can have ready is a supply of 'filler' remarks, such as the phrase: *Don't expect me to pay for that!* which was mentioned earlier. Think about what suits you and store such phrases away: you will inevitably need something like it on occasion.

So, the response to accidents should not be all doom and gloom, they may present a chance to shine. Out-and-out accidents are not the only thing you will have to cope with and another category of occurrence is worth a separate word.

Unforeseen incidents

There is certainly an overlap here, but the heading implies a different kind of event. Thus a different kind of response may be called for when there is an *accident*: these can sometimes be the speaker's fault (for example, you drop something) or the cause is far removed from the group (for instance, a fire alarm rings in a hotel meeting room) as opposed to what is defined here as an *incident* where others may be involved.

An example will make the point. For instance, imagine that a speaker is proceeding well. Let us say they are presenting a plan to the Board of Directors, when the meeting room door opens and a secretary or assistant enters with a tray of tea. What should the speaker do? Consider:

- •)) Should the speaker continue?

- •)) Will the noise (of cups and saucers being laid out) be a distraction? A serious one?

- •)) The group is senior (the Board), would it be impolite to stop or complain?

- •)) Was it organised for it to happen at this time?

- •)) Could it be a mistake, perhaps the meeting should have been left undisturbed?

There is, I believe, an important rule here: *never compete with an interruption*. It will always distract and always dilute the effectiveness of what you are doing. This means that the first response to such an incident should be to acknowledge it. The *intention* must be to:

- •)) Ensure it is clear you are not unaware of the problem (someone may well be wondering what the matter is with a speaker who carries on as if no-one is distracted when clearly they are)

- •)) Either minimise or eliminate the interruption

- •)) Summon assistance if appropriate

- •)) Maintain the overall smooth flow of the presentation as far as possible

- •)) Reinforce the capability of the speaker (recovering well even from minor mishaps is often well regarded, especially by those who judge they would not have done so well faced with something similar).

Consider these issues further by reference to our example. For instance, consider what options the tea delivery mentioned above might pose:

- •)) Simply acknowledging it may remove it (*Perhaps the serving of the tea could wait just a few minutes until we are finished* – whoever is doing the delivery may, hearing this, beat a hasty retreat. In some groups a moment's silence might well have the same effect)

- •)) Asking the Chair (if there is one) for a view (*Would you like me to pause for a moment while the tea is laid out?* – this may prompt a number of useful responses: from agreement that you should do so, to an instruction that the tea should wait)

- •)) Adjust your timing so that you can break earlier than planned (*I see the tea is here. Let's break now therefore and I will pick up the point…*)

Remember that it may well be necessary to complete the sentence or the point being made immediately before the event prior to interrupting to take action as described above. It may also be wise to recap a little if you break and resume later, even if the gap is slight.

Note: one regular hazard these days is the ubiquitous mobile phone. A reminder to turn them off is appropriate in many gatherings and the 'never compete with an interruption' advice stands: if one rings, wait until it is silenced, perhaps saying something like, *Can't be for me, mine's switched off.*

Some things are so serious that there is little alternative but to stop for a while; for instance if nothing can be heard without the microphone and it goes dead.

Both these kinds of thing, accidents and incidents, are exceptions. Do not fret about the possibility throughout a talk, but bear in mind that successful recovery makes a good impression and that forewarned is forearmed.

Try it

> Certainly you should think about such things in advance and have a few thoughts in mind. In rehearsing a talk you might decide on a particular possible interruption and incorporate dealing with it into your practice. One colleague of mine tells me he has done this using an electric kitchen timer. He gives it a turn – without looking accurately at the time it is set for – and then regards the ensuing buzz as an interruption and practises recovering from it.

Three further topics need addressing before this chapter is finished. These are timing, what I call 'flourishes' and the use of humour.

Timing

I say, I say, I say what is the secret of perfect comedy?

I don't know, what is … *Timing.*

It is an old joke, but in virtually all kinds of presentation, timing, in the sense of time-keeping, is important. Like punctuality, which acts in part as a courtesy and saves wasting time, especially other people's time, good time-keeping shows respect for the group. To keep your options open, you may promise little else about what you do during your talk, but keeping to time should be one promise that is always fulfilled.

In certain circumstances time-keeping is one of a number of factors that will be taken as indicative of your attitude to things. It is a courtesy and a sign of professionalism. At an important function, if you are allocated half an hour, then you sit down after twenty-eight minutes. If you run over, you immediately lose part of the audience's attention as they think to themselves, *How much longer than the set time is this going to take?* Run wildly over and the audience may take bets on when you will finally stop, especially if they are not finding the proceedings interesting.

If you are looking to impress people then good time-keeping is one sure way to boost the impression you give. It is impressive precisely because it is difficult, so it is worth working to achieve.

So, having established that it is important – how do you keep to time? The following summarise some facts that help, and in some cases link to points made earlier:

- •)) Use your notes to judge time, knowing how long a page in your particular style represents (you also can flag particular points: half-way, at what time you should start to summarise and so on)

- •)) Rehearse and time it, particularly where timing is key, it will help ensure accuracy

- •)) Keep an eye on the time (with your watch on the table in front of you – you might ask someone else to give you signals but they are not always reliable)

- •)) Have some options in your material, elements that can be added or dropped to match the time you are in effect taking

- •)) Take note of how long your talks take. If you aim at twenty minutes and run to only fifteen or to twenty-five, make a note of why and learn from the experience

- •)) Allow for contingency, think about how much of the time will go on the introduction from the Chair, the coffee break or questions and so on

All these are things that may help. Again do not despair: it does get easier to judge with practice over time and while you will not always get it exactly right, if you work at it, you will have a reasonable chance of coming close.

As a final thought here, the discipline of good time-keeping by the speaker sets an example. It is little use chastising people for returning late after a coffee break, or failing to be ready to start on time, if they know your own attempts at time-keeping are a joke.

A flourish

The next heading in this chapter refers to something which both shows how a number of the techniques discussed here can usefully work together to enhance their effect, and also adds an extra dimension. Let me explain with some examples:

•)) One kind of flourish (difficult to exemplify on the page without hearing it) is simply when at a key point the emphasis and meaning are exactly and very apparently right. Rather as the punch line of a good funny story must be just right, so a phrase, a summary or key point comes over to perfection. This may involve finding just the right turn of phrase, delivering it with just the right emphasis and timing and with a matching gesture that suits the moment, and carrying it out with apparent natural ease. It is, if you like, a peak of the animation that needs to constantly enliven any address. As such it is an exceptional moment. The whole talk cannot be like this, though some talks need, by their nature, more of this factor than others. Sometimes a particular passage simply lends itself to this and inspiration fires it up as it is delivered. On other occasions the effect is well planned; sometimes too, it combines a little of both. Listen to how politicians speak at something like a party conference as they regularly finish a point with a sentence that says, *Isn't that true, isn't it well put? Applaud now.*

•)) Another kind of flourish involves an appropriate (again usually but not always thought out) 'event' that is added specifically to enliven. For example, I was once in the audience at a meeting where one speaker made a dramatic start: *Ladies and Gentlemen*, he began, *I know time is short, but in the hour I have available I will …* The Chairman, who sat beside him, looked horrified, tugged his sleeve and pointed to his watch. The speaker glanced in his direction for a second, and continued: *Of course, I am so sorry*, he said, *In the half an hour I am allocated…* As he said this he paused, lifted his notes, in the form of A4 sheets, and tore them in half lengthways down the page, thus apparently halving the duration of his talk. He then continued – with every member of the group giving him their complete attention. The feeling in the room said, *This should be good.*

•)) On another occasion I saw someone involve a member of the group he was addressing to create such a flourish. He was setting out some changes in policy affecting budgets. There were cutbacks and much carping about certain expenses, now disallowed, though as someone had said it was: *only a fiver.* He asked if anyone had a five pound note. Someone handed one over. He promptly tore it up, sprinkling the pieces across the table to the clear horror of the volunteer. *But it's only a fiver,* he said going on to contrast the attitude of many people towards what they see as 'company' money or 'my' money. It made a dramatic point (though it cost him a fiver! – as he did repay the money later). I have some worthless South American notes I keep for similar purposes.

•)) Even so small a thing as a man removing his jacket (suggesting informality or a workshop environment) can inspire confidence. I saw this done once in two stages: first the jacket was removed, then the braces that were revealed as a result. It got a chuckle and made a point.

Such actions need an element of creativity, but you can plan their inclusion in what you do. There are, of course, dangers here. There is nothing worse than a dramatic gesture that falls flat so you need to progress with some care; I once saw someone fail to make a magic trick work. Embarrassing. The more complicated or dramatic something is the more sure you must be that it will work. The combining of a number of factors, both verbal and physical, to create particular impact is something that adds to the overall impression a speaker makes. When done well it is seamless. In other words, the whole thing flows smoothly along, there is variety of pace and emphasis and an occasional flourish is reached, smoothly and naturally executed as a high point in the presentation's progress, then the flow continues. The intention is for the emphasis achieved to be more striking than the method of achieving it.

A flourish may include another factor as yet unmentioned, that of humour.

A funny thing

Humour is invaluable for varying the pace, changing the mood, providing an interval and – perhaps more important – reinforcing a point. Most talks are improved by a light moment, and some speeches – at a wedding, for instance – contain an intentional and significant amount of humour.

But ... humour is a funny business and needs sensitive handling; it should not be overdone. It was Noël Coward who said: *Wit ought to be a glorious treat, like caviar; never spread it around like marmalade.* This last sentence is designed to illustrate just how humour can work in a presentation. It does not have to make people roll around laughing. The quote above is mildly amusing but cleverly put, and reminds me of another quote: *When a thing has been said and said well, have no scruple. Take it and copy it* (Anatole France). Sorry – I'm digressing again.

Actually quotations are a useful way to inject a lighter touch to your speaking. There are many books of quotations, often focusing on particular areas from humorous ones to those that relate only to business or travel or whatever. In addition, and if you like to use the internet, you may like to check out www.cyber-nation.com a site which, apparently just because someone there likes them, lists the best part of 50,000 quotations and will let you add your favourites.

Such things certainly provide a light moment, but they can make a point too with what they say. Most business presentations are not appropriate to a great deal of hilarity, but many can usefully include a smile or two. And some may have a more social connotation and need more, as with say a retirement party: *I well remember the day John started work here. I overheard two of the girls in the Accounts office talking about him. One said: 'Doesn't that Mr Green dress well' and the other replied, 'Yes and so quickly'.*

Humour is, however, difficult to judge. What one group may laugh out loud at raises not a murmur from another, and there is nothing so likely to knock your confidence as an out-and-out joke that falls flat. Back to Noël Coward, because a quotation has some safety built in, particularly if it contains clear content or a moral. People may only smile inwardly for a moment at such a phrase, but it lifts the proceedings and varies the pace, perhaps also having a positive effect on the rapport being established between the speaker and the audience.

If you want to be sure of raising a serious smile or an outright laugh then the humour must be tested, something that you know from past experience works. It is often more important for it to be successful, and pertinent, than for it to be original.

Short, witty injections, of which quotes are but one example, work better in many circumstances than long stories. If a longer story does not work, or even does not work particularly well, then it can act to dilute the whole effectiveness of what is being done. Because of this it is usually better to include any humour as an aside rather than as a big production number. If it does not work very well then no matter, you can quickly move on. If it has a moral, then that may make a mark without needing to prove very humorous, and this may still work fine. So think very carefully before you say something like, *This will make you laugh ...* How you introduce such an aside needs careful attention in light of the role humour has and how it affects matters.

The link to the topic is important. Examples in print are not the same as something delivered in the right way 'on the day'; however, let me risk an example of the smile rather than belly-laugh variety. Again it is a quote: the late Isaac Asimov, the well-known and prolific science and science fiction writer (he wrote more than 400 books), was once asked what he would do if he heard he only had six months to live. He thought for a moment, and replied in just two words: *Type faster.* I quote this sometimes when talking about business writing skills and it certainly raises a smile. More important it links well to that topic, showing the power of language, how just two words can say so much about someone, their attitudes to their work, their readers and more. Yet such a small digression does not disrupt the flow or take over the proceedings, and such a thing can quickly be glossed over if you pick something that works less well than you would like. Some people commend the idea of having back-up comments to use noted in your running guide. If your first quip falls a little flat you can rapidly add a further, better, comment, though beware of digging the hole deeper if more than one does not work well.

Again this is not an area on which to overstretch yourself. If the only appropriate story you can think of needs an accurate foreign accent to make it work, omit it if the accent is outside your repertoire. If timing is not your forte or if you can never remember a punch line, avoid anything complex or work from an especially clear note. Some stories or quips have a potential awkwardness about them in terms of delivery. For example, one business quip I like is about the man who discovered the perfect business venture to make big profits: he sets out to purchase MBAs for what they were worth, and sell them for what they *think* they are worth. Nothing elaborate and it will not engender more than a quiet smile, but you do have to get such a thing the right way round! What is seemingly simple in print can become ridiculously tongue-tying on your feet at a key moment in your presentation – this is just the sort of thing that should be completely clear in any note you have in front of you.

The not a joke story

There are various categories of story that can be used to good effect, fitting with a topic and raising at least a smile. Here are two example of what one might call classic tales. The first could fit in if optimism is being referred to in a speech:

I will, I will, I will ...

There is a tale from medieval times about a servant in the King's household who is condemned to life imprisonment for some small misdemeanour. Languishing in his cell, a thought struck him and he sent a message to the King promising that, if he were released, he would work day and night and, within a year, he would teach the King's favourite horse to talk.

This amused the King, and he ordered the servant to be released to work in the Royal stables. The servant's friends were at once pleased to see him released, yet frightened for him too; after all, horses do not talk, however much training they get.

'What will you do?', they all asked.

'So much can happen in a year', he replied. 'I may die, the King may die, or – who knows – the horse may talk!'

Who knows indeed; I for one hope that by the time the year was up he had thought of another ruse.

The second fits with many business topics and can act as a cautionary note to stress the need for practicality:

The lion and the wolf ...

Once upon a time ... there was a wolf. He was scruffy, bedraggled and generally down at heel. He scratched a living where he could, but was regarded by the other animals as very low in the pecking order. He hated this; he wanted to be well regarded and, after long fruitless hours trying to think how he could change his image, he concluded he needed help. He asked an aardvark, an anteater and an antelope for advice. Nothing; though the antelope suggested that he should ask the lion – *after all he's the king of the jungle*. Risky it might be, but he was desperate, so he went and – very carefully – approached the lion, saying:

'I want people to like me, I don't want to be thought of as just a scruffy lowlife; I want to be loved. What can I do? Please advise me, your Majesty.'

The lion was irritated by the interruption but he paused and gave it a moment's thought.

'You should become a bunny rabbit,' said the lion, 'everyone loves a bunny rabbit. I think it's the long floppy ears and the big eyes. Yes, that's it – become a bunny rabbit.'

The wolf did the wolf equivalent of touching his forelock, thanked the lion and slunk away. But almost at once he thought – Wait a minute, how do I become a bunny rabbit? So, he went back, risked interrupting the lion again and said:

'Sorry … excuse me, it is, of course, a wonderful idea of yours this business of my becoming a bunny rabbit, but … but how exactly do I do that?'

The lion drew himself up to his full height, ruffled his mane and said simply:

'As king of the jungle, I'm concerned with strategy – *how* you do it is for you to work out.'

Despite the *caveats* stated here, humour is an important element of many a presentation. It can act to break the ice early on, to change the mood, to provide a memorable image to augment, or assist retention of, the message, and can contain a moral or truth that is very much part of the message. In addition you may want to have a quip or two up your sleeve for use as 'fillers' or in response to incidents, for example greeting an interrupting mobile telephone ring with: *I keep telling her not to ring me here,* before making a more practical comment to deal with it. Sometimes circumstances make for effortless humour. Once when speaking in a hotel meeting room, we were conscious of a meeting going on next door. Most of the time we heard nothing, but were aware that people were there. At one point I made a remark that produced some laughter in the room. This was coincidentally followed immediately by a burst of laughter from next door where something similar had presumably happened. I had the presence of mind to say something like: *I didn't think it was that funny, and besides I didn't even know they could hear us,* getting another laugh before we moved on.

I keep meaning to record more systematically than I do stories I have heard, used and found useful. I know some people who do so systematically and are never stuck for an appropriate tale. Appropriate includes the vexed question of good taste. Horses for courses; but in public there are occasions when it is usually best to keep off anything sensitive, such as sex, religion or politics. You only have to upset one member of a group to sound a sour note. Remember that if you tell a story with a double meaning then it can only mean one thing. Always keep in mind the nature of the group, consider what you know about them and work from that.

If you do not want to be seen as delivering verbal Mogadon, you will need to use some humour at least occasionally. As a further example, and to provide a light-hearted end to this chapter, let me quote one story I stole and used on a company conference to lead in to a serious review of financial resources:

A smart, new, top-of-the-range Volvo 4x4 estate, boot full of expensive riding gear, tow bar, driven by a very smart rather 'county' lady is attempting – very inexpertly – to park in the last space in a car park. She goes to and fro, but cannot get the angle right. Then, as she backs up to try again for the twenty-seventh time, a small flashy sporting saloon of the kind that comes with built-in bumptiousness and with a driver to match, nips through the gap into the space.

The driver gets out and, as he locks the door, cannot resist shouting to the Volvo driver: *That's what you can do if you can drive properly.* The Volvo driver slips the automatic gear change into reverse, puts her foot hard on the accelerator and rams her car back hard into the sports car, the tow bar digging deeply into the metal with a sickening crunch. In the silence that follows, the lady winds down the window and calls over: *And that, young man, is what you can do if you have money!*

The old ones are often the best! And this can be made to link neatly to a number of topics. As an aside, I would mention that if you want to investigate the area of using humour further, then perhaps I might offer a totally biased recommendation and suggest you see my book, *Hook your audience*, published by Management Pocketbooks. The Volvo story is one of a number of examples in that book.

But humour always remains an area about which to plan with some care. Just one small hazard is how you reference something like this. I once remember coming to the words 'Volvo story' in my notes and at that moment having no clue as to what it meant. The moral is to make clear notes that you will always understand. So take care: I always remember a rhyme about after-dinner speaking said by the humorist Dennis Norden:

> *I am gentle by nature, not stormy*
>
> *But a dam inside of me broke*
>
> *When the man who was speaking before me*
>
> *Wound up with my opening joke.*

CHAPTER 6

Worth a Thousand Words

Seeing is believing.

Traditional proverb

You cannot just speak. Any kind of public speech is, in part, visual. It is a truism about the way people take in information that seeing as well as hearing makes getting and maintaining attention more likely. This means that, if circumstances allow, then it is a good idea to have something visual alongside what you say.

Perhaps the most important visual aid has already been mentioned: it is you. Numbers of factors, such as simple gestures (for example, a hand pointing), and more dramatic ones like banging a fist on the table, which I like to describe as flourishes are part of this, as is your general manner and appearance.

All sorts of things can be used as visual aids. A picture is said to be worth a thousand words. Certainly a picture can largely speak for itself, and it may be in many forms: a painting, a photograph (black and white or colour), a line drawing or cartoon. A well-chosen illustration can make an otherwise bland point memorable. A cartoon is one form: I used to have a slide, which I used when talking about efficiency and time management in the workplace. It showed a manager sitting at his office desk, a secretary is standing beside him holding some papers and saying, *Do you want this again, or shall I file it?* Amusing, yet it makes a good point – too many managers regard filing as a way of getting things off their desk, and do not think of the consequences or cost of storing an ever-growing volume of paper. As an aside, remember that many such things, published in a magazine say, are copyright and should not be used as a slide without permission.

At my daughter's wedding a projected montage of photographs of her and her new husband as children acted as a backdrop to the wedding breakfast and speeches. In a business context I once saw someone who was talking about mining produce a substantial piece of rock: he described it as some of the hardest rock on the planet, then turned it towards the audience and showed as well as described how the equipment he was talking about had cut through it 'like a knife through butter' leaving a flat, smooth surface as testament to the equipment's prowess.

Items can be produced from a pocket (money); larger things from below the table or behind a lectern (a bottle of wine) or even unveiled rather as at an official ceremony (like a sheet being pulled from over a life-sized cardboard cut-out photograph of a person). Anything like this can work well, and, of course, it works best when it has real relevance and is not just 'clever'.

But more traditional forms of visual aid are also important. Such things as slides serve several purposes, including:

- •)) Focusing attention within the group

- •)) Helping change pace, add variety and so on

- •)) Giving a literally visual aspect to something

- •)) Acting as signposts to where within the structure the presentation has reached.

Some, especially slides, also help you keep track, providing reminders over and above your speaker's notes on what comes next.

Be careful. Visual aids should *support* the message, not lead or take it over. Just because slides exist or are easy to originate does not mean they will be right. You need to start by looking at the message, at what you are trying to do, and see what will help put it over and have an additive effect. They may make a point that is difficult or impossible to describe, in the way a graph might make an instant point which might otherwise be lost in a mass of figures. As an example here, the simple pie chart in Figure 8 below, makes a clear point about the need to think about how much of a presentation comes over to the audience through the visuals and how much through the person doing the presenting. This may also make a useful image to keep in mind as you prepare and then give talks.

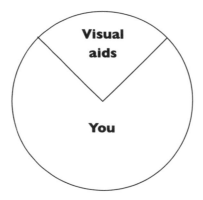

FIGURE 8: *Influences on how you come over*

Whatever your reasons for using visual aids, and you may have a particular reason to use them, they help, perhaps, to get a large amount of information over more quickly. However, you do need to use them in just the right way.

The checklist that follows deals, briefly, with the various options, offers general guidance on the production and use of visual aids, and some tips on using the ubiquitous overhead projector (OHP) and PowerPoint. A further checklist at the end of this chapter sets out and compares the advantages and disadvantages of the main methods.

General principles of using visual aids

•))) Keep the content simple

•))) Restrict the amount of information and the number of words:

- Use single words to give structure, headings, or short statements

- Avoid a cluttered, fussy or complicated look

- Use a running logo (like a main heading/topic on each slide)

Without a doubt the worst, and commonest, fault in using visual aids is to pack them so full of information as to make them more confusing than illuminating. More of this anon.

•))) Use diagrams, graphs and the like where possible rather than too many numbers; and never read figures aloud without visual support

•))) Build in variety within the overall theme: for example, with colour or variations of the form of aid used

•))) Emphasise the theme and structure: for example, regularly using a single aid to recap the agenda or objectives

•))) Ensure the content of the visual matches the words you will use (so, for example, do not put the word logistics on a slide and then talk only about timing – it leaves people unsure quite where you are)

•))) Make sure all content is necessary and relevant (a common fault is the use of existing items – a graph or page from a report, perhaps – and then ignoring most of what is there, focusing on one aspect of it only. People can see the rest, however, and part of their mind is distracted wondering what it is all about)

•)) Ensure everything is visible: asking yourself: is it clear? will it work in the room? does it suit the equipment? (colours, and the right sized typeface help here)

•)) Ensure the layout emphasises the meaning you want (and not some minor detail)

•)) Pick the right aid for the right purpose.

Using any sort of visual aid needs a little orchestrating. It can be awkward initially to have to speak, keep your place, remember to show something and actually organise to do so. The answer is easy: take a moment and do not allow the process to rattle you. If people cannot see what you are doing, and frankly even if they can, just bridge any slight gap in the content of what you are saying with a descriptive comment – *The next slide illustrates this, let me just show you.* In the time you take to say even that much what you have to do will likely be done.

More than one US President has been accused of being unable to think and chew gum at the same time. But if you prefer to keep silent for a moment, let us say as you write something up on a flipchart or an overhead projector, so be it – no-one will mind, especially if it is preceded by a brief comment of explanation. Saying one thing and writing something else simultaneously is complicated, and it is much better to take a moment to get it right than try to do two things at once and stumble.

The two most commonly used ways of projecting slides are now the overhead projector and PowerPoint, which is rapidly overtaking it in use. There are other things, of course, such as 35 mm slides (though that changes the feel of a presentation as the lights need turning down for people to see and any visual elements projected by the speaker disappear). We will take these in turn.

Using an overhead projector (OHP)

Some care should be taken in using an overhead projector to begin with; they appear deceptively simple, but present inherent hazards to the unwary. The following hints may well be useful:

- •)) Make sure the electric flex is out of the way (or taped to the floor); falling over it will improve neither your presentation nor your dignity

- •)) Make sure it works before you start using it with the group (this goes for the second bulb – and a spare, even – and the roll of acetate film if you are using one)

- •)) Make sure it is positioned where you want; within reach, and giving you room to move and space alongside for papers (*note:* it may need to be in a slightly different place for left/right handed people – a hazard for some team presentations)

- •)) Stand back and to the side of it: be sure not to obscure the view of the screen for anyone in the group

- •)) Having made sure the picture is in focus, look primarily at the machine and not the screen – the OHP's primary advantage is to keep you facing the front

- •)) Only use slides that have big enough typefaces or images and, if you plan to write on acetate, check how large your handwriting needs to be

- •)) Switch off when changing slides; it looks more professional than the jumbled image that appears as slides are changed while the unit is switched on

- •)) If you want to project the image on a slide progressively you can cover the bottom part of the image with a sheet of paper (placed over the slide on the machine). Use paper that is not too thick and you will still be able to see the whole image through it even though the whole image is not projected. As you slide the paper down it may be useful to put a weight on it, otherwise it reaches the point where it must be held or it will drop off

•))) For hand-written use an acetate roll (fitted running from the back to the front of the machine) minimises the amount of acetate used (it is expensive) and removes the need to keep changing loose sheets. Things can be written as you go, or ahead of your starting; if you need to draw something like a circle, then this might sensibly be done ahead to ensure it is neat

•))) Remember that when something new is shown, all attention is, at least momentarily, on it – so always pause for a moment as something is revealed, or what you say may be missed

•))) It may be useful to add emphasis by highlighting certain things on the slides as you go through them; if you slip the slide under the acetate roll you can do this without adjustment and without marking the slide

•))) Similarly, two slides shown together can add information (or you can use overlays attached to the slide and folded across); alternatively, the second slide may have minimal information on it, with such things as a title talk, session heading, or company logo remaining in view on one as others are shown by being placed over it

•))) If you want to point something out and highlight it, then this is most easily done by laying a small pointer (or pencil) on the projector. Extending pointers are, in my view, almost impossible to use without appearing pretentious, and they risk you turning your back on the group unnecessarily.

The OHP remains a very useful device and will no doubt be used a while longer, despite the continuing revolution in computers.

PowerPoint

This, and to be fair other systems as well, allows you to prepare slides on your computer and present them through a projector using the computer to control the show. So far so good. It works well and you have the ability to use a variety of layouts, colours, illustrations and so on at the touch of a button.

There are some dangers (and many of the points made in reviewing the use of an OHP apply equally here). First, do not let the technology carry you away. Not everything it will do is useful – certainly not all on one slide or even in one presentation – and, as has been said, it is a common error to allow the ease of preparation to increase the amount of information on a slide beyond the point where it becomes cluttered and difficult to follow. This might also lead you to use too many slides. Similarly, if you are going to use its various features, like the ability to introduce one line and then subsequent ones to make up a full picture, remember to keep whatever is done manageable. Details here can be important, for instance colour choice is prodigious but not all are equally suitable for making things clear.

The second danger is simply the increased risk of technological complexity. Sometimes this produces a simple error. Recently I saw an important presentation have to proceed without the planned slides because the projector (resident at the venue) could not be connected to the laptop computer (which had been brought to the venue) because the leads were incompatible. Sometimes problems may be caused by something buried in the software. Again not long ago I sat through a presentation that used twenty or thirty slides, and each time the slide was changed there was an unplanned delay of three or four seconds. It was felt unwarranted to stop and risk tinkering with the equipment, but long before the three-quarters of an hour presentation finished everyone in the group found it disproportionately maddening.

So make sure (check, check, check ...) that everything is going to work. Run off transparencies that can be shown on an OHP in the event of disaster striking if this would be a sensible insurance (or a paper handout copy). Finally follow all the overall rules and always bear in mind that you do not have to have a slide on all the time – when you have finished with one, blank out the screen until you are ready for the next slide (just press the B key, and continue by pressing it again).

Whatever you use, remember to talk to the audience and not to the visual aid. Looking over your shoulder at the screen too much when slides are used is a common fault. Make sure visuals are visible (do not get in the way yourself), explain them or their purpose as necessary, mention whether or not people will get a paper copy of them and stop them distracting the audience by removing them as soon as you are finished with them.

Is it one of Murphy's Laws? Certainly it is an accurate maxim that if something can go wrong it will; and nowhere is this truer than with electrical and IT equipment.

The moral: check, check and check again. Everything – from the spare OHP bulb (do not even think about using an old machine with only one bulb) to which way up 35mm slides are going to be and what you need to make more sophisticated equipment work – even whether the pens for the flipchart still work – is worth checking.

Always double-check anything with which you are unfamiliar, especially if, like with a microphone for instance, what you do is going to be significantly dependent on it. And remember that while the sophistication of equipment increases all the time, so too do the number of things that can potentially go wrong.

The concept of contingency is worth a thought; what do you do if disaster does strike? You have been warned.

The dangers of standardisation

PowerPoint is now ubiquitous. The system is in almost every computer. Literally tens of millions of people use it – and do so around the globe. It makes creating simple slides easy, but it also standardises to a worrying extent.

Imagine: He who must be listened to stands at the front of the room, surrounded by equipment and with the screen glowing behind him. The audience is spellbound. The little company logo at the corner of the screen fascinates them. Every time the presenter clicks the computer mouse, and sends another yellow bullet point shuttling onto the screen from stage left, their attention soars. One slide replaces another, then another replaces that and another … but you get the idea. Enough. All are bland, all are simple checklists, yet he who must be listened to finds them riveting; certainly he spends most of his time looking over his shoulder at the screen rather than at the audience. There is so much text on some slides that they are like pages out of a book. And an unsuitably small typeface compounds the effect and overburdens the minds of the audience. The figure that follows shows this standardisation graphically. So he reads them, verbatim, more slowly than the audience does and with a tone that leads one to suspect that he is seeing them for the first time. It becomes akin to a bureaucratic rain dance: a mantra and format is slavishly, indeed unthinkingly, followed – yet at the end no-one is truly satisfied. The opportunity – the open goal – is missed.

The main heading

· This is a bullet point

· This is another

· This is another

· This is one more

· And this is yet another

· And this is a bullet point as well

· And this ... but you get the idea

Figure 9: *Example slide*

If only good business presentations were that easy, so mechanistic: put up one slide read everything crammed onto it out loud – repeat slide by slide, and success follows automatically. But they are not. Large numbers of lacklustre, wordy slides do not a good presentation make. Certainly they do not make a distinctive or memorable one. But then perhaps, honestly assessed, he who must be listened to did not really believe they did so. The slides are there – be honest – because that is how presentations are prepared. A ubiquitous norm is followed largely unthinkingly, and the results fail to sparkle. Indeed they may fail to explain, inform and certainly to persuade.

It is worth suggesting care too with the equally ubiquitous ClipArt: again this is on most computers and allows you to select little illustrations and slot them into the corner of a slide, which would otherwise show only words. Too often the illustrations chosen only add a modicum of something visual, they are trite, only loosely linked to the text and add little or nothing to the totality of the slide that they are on. They are picked out as a routine, and little thought is involved. Moreover, the same images can become overused and everyone has seen them before.

Audiences may put up with all this, and a comparison with the norm of their experience may not be so bad, but everyone is aware that something is missing.

Signs of a revolt

Such a by-the-book approach, screening out any real, individual consideration of what is best, is so prevalent amongst PowerPoint users and so ill thought of by those on the receiving end of such presentations that it has become subject of academic and journalistic comment, and coined the phrase: *death by PowerPoint*. And it is the slides used that come in for the greatest criticism.

For instance, in America a well-known and respected academic, Edward R Tufte of Yale, who is a communications expert, has written a strong condemnation of PowerPoint, in his article *'The Cognitive Style of PowerPoint'* (which you can read in full by accessing www.edwardtufte.com). One fascinating example he uses concerns the Columbia space shuttle disaster. In a slide presentation, which Tufte calls, *an exercise in misdirection*, a crucial piece of information in which the foam section that detached and crippled the craft is described as 640 times larger than ones which reassuring pre-flight advice described, was buried in small type several layers down in a packed PowerPoint list. Though danger was actually flagged, the warning it gave was not noticed. The main heading on the slide indicated a positive outcome to tests, saying: 'Review of Test Data indicates Conservatism for Tile Penetration'. One might criticise the language too, but the point remains – the key information was passed over unnoticed.

To reinforce any lingering feeling that traditional PowerPoint style and practice are fine, try looking at www.norvig.com/Gettysburg where Peter Norvig has posted a wonderful spoof of Abraham Lincoln's Gettysburg address:

Four score and seven years ago our fathers brought forth on this continent a new nation, conceived in liberty and dedicated to the proposition that all men are created equal.

Such stirring language and thoughts are reduced to banality by a visual presentation that is not visual, and which uses bullet points such as 'Met on battlefield (great)'. As an example of how to reduce a powerful and memorable message to insignificance; this is a classic.

In Britain, a recent feature by John Naughton in a serious newspaper, *The Guardian*, addressed the same issue, quoted Tufte's American article and added its own despairing spin: *Power corrupts. PowerPoint obfuscates. Next time you have to give a presentation, leave it at home.*

The reasons why such comment is made is obvious: the prevailing style of PowerPoint driven presentations, while they are something audiences expect and tolerate, do not satisfy many audiences as they should. A good, stylish presenter, with presence and panache, may be able to make up for this – but only in part.

Go back to the essential rules set out above. Too much text is the worst mistake; it blights too many presentations, especially those made using PowerPoint. PowerPoint can do extraordinary things, buried in that seemingly simple piece of software is a resource that can produce visuals that are striking, full of colour, movement and images and which truly deserve the term 'visual aid'. The full potential of this is somewhat beyond our brief here, but if you are interested check out the book *Killer Presentations*, which I wrote with Nick Oulton. His organisation, m62 Visual Communications, is a leader in this field, so much so that it has been described thus: *These guys know more about PowerPoint than anybody else on the face of the planet* by the vice president of IT giant Symantic. Its focus is on marketing presentations, but the description and illustrations of what can be done simply amazes many people (the book also provides links to Nick's website so that readers can see a moving presentation as they read about it).

Having said all that, I do not have the intention to put you off using PowerPoint, or indeed any other similar system. It is only to emphasise the need for some thought about it and particularly to flag the danger of doing any of this as a routine – working, if you like, on automatic pilot.

As a dramatic example of the way in which the automatic pilot operates – the rut it can put you in is a deep one – consider the following example, one quoted in my book *Marketing and Selling Professional Services* [Kogan Page]. It concerns a sales pitch for which a firm of architects involved prepared slides to show to the committee of a charity for the blind. They really did not think of the audience – but just blindly (I know) followed the routine of how their presentations were always prepared and based it on a battery of slides and pictures. The absurdity of it only dawned on them minutes before the presentation was due to start, when they found that ten of the twelve strong committee were blind. As the managing director of the firm told me as I prepared a workshop for them: *If that can be overlooked, anything can be overlooked.* This may seem fantastic, but it really is true and provides testimony to the power – and danger – of operating on automatic pilot, of just sailing unthinkingly into some preordained way of preparing something. The same effect no doubt produces all too many similar, if lesser, disasters or mishaps.

Anything and everything

Finally, it pays to adopt an inventive approach here. As has been said, practically anything can act as a visual aid, from another person (carefully briefed to play their part) to an exhibit of some sort. In a business presentation, exhibits may be obvious items: products, samples, posters etc. or may be something totally unexpected. Something unexpected, surprising and striking can have considerable impact.

Conversely, if something complicated is necessary, then it may work best as a handout – everyone can look at their personal copy, take in the detail and then relate it to what is being said.

Externally there are hotels and conference centres whose proud boast is that access and strength allow you to say: *What we need now is some really heavyweight support* – as the baby elephant actually walks across the platform behind you. The possibilities with visual aids are virtually endless.

Like all the skills involved in making presentations, while the basics give you a sound foundation, the process is something that can benefit from a little imagination.

Now, a final promised checklist before we move on.

Checklist: different methods of visualisation compared

Flipcharts

Advantages

No power source needed

Can be prepared beforehand

Can be adapted/amended as you go

Easy to see

Available at many venues

Easy to write on (use sufficiently large writing)

Can use different colours

You can refer back and forward

Disadvantages

Expensive to prepare professionally

Large and awkward to move

Masking is difficult/messy

Poor handwriting spoils effect

Overall

Makes a better work pad than a means of presenting pre-prepared information.

Fixed white board

Advantages

Available at many venues

Useful work pad

If metal backed will allow magnets to hold paper

Disadvantages

Needs special pens (Be careful! A venue will not be pleased if you use permanent pens on one)

Poor handwriting can spoil effect

Erasing takes longer than turning a page on a flipchart

Overall

Another good work pad

Overhead projector (OHP)

Advantages

Can be seen in a brightly lit room

Produces a large image

Masking is easily possible (allowing a message to be revealed progressively)

Slides can be pre-prepared, reused and are easily transported

Looks professional

Available at many venues

Slides act as prompt (and information on frames is visible to the speaker but not to the audience)

Disadvantages

Needs a power source

Can be noisy (fan)

A little obtrusive standing between the speaker and audience

Can break down

Requires a screen or suitable wall to project onto

Needs getting used to if speaker is to appear professional

Overall

Good as a prepared base for slides, but with acetate sheets or roll can act as a work pad as well. Can project pictures, maybe not as well as 35mm slide projector – but does so without having to have the room darkened, something that rules out 35mm slides for many uses as the speaker effectively disappears.

PowerPoint

This is now increasingly used instead of an OHP. It has many of the same advantages and disadvantages. Full use of the software can produce awesome images, but origination takes time, may need training and can be very expensive if done professionally. The chances of something going wrong increase as the technology is complex. Normally all is well, but use needs care, preparation and some people feel safest with back-up (for example, slides also printed off ready to run on an OHP in case a problem develops).

Overall

The methodology of choice for so many things; anyone speaking regularly at events probably needs some familiarity with this.

Handouts

Advantages

Can look professional

Allows specific detailed points to be looked at

Good for technical information

Disadvantages

Temptation to use too much information

Can distract more easily from verbal presentation (and cannot be easily removed after use)

Overall

Has its place for certain types of information

May also distract as they are distributed

Next, as well as showing things to your audience, you may need to involve them in other ways.

CHAPTER 7

Involving the Audience

The best audience is intelligent, well educated and a little drunk

Alben W Barkley

As has been stressed throughout, audiences are important; but they should never be regarded simply as a passive target. They may sometimes need – or demand – to be involved. Certainly there should always be a link with them. Eye contact has been mentioned in Chapter 5. The feedback that comes from it and from general observation of the sound and signs of the group and from individual members of it are always going to underpin any involvement with the audience.

In small groups, presentations may sometimes be only a step removed from a round table meeting. A manager at the head of a boardroom table, or the Chair of a committee, may be on their feet and presenting, yet still engage individual members of the group in individual exchanges – to obtain more pointed and immediate feedback perhaps: *What is your view of this, Mary?* Too far in this direction takes us into training or perhaps counselling rather than simply presentation or speech making. Here, in the context of formal presentations, involvement is taken to mean the process of encouraging, where that is necessary or desirable, and dealing with, questions.

So, how do we deal with this? In three stages, considering:

- •)) when to take questions

- •)) how to prompt them when desired

- •)) and then how to answer them.

When to take questions

The first thing to be said here is that the option to decide when to take questions may not be that of the speaker. If an invitation to speak is issued, then the format of the meeting may well be fixed. This is as likely to be the case both internally within an organisation or externally. Always find out what the format of a particular meeting is, and if you think some variant would be better (either for you or for the meeting) *consider* asking whoever is in charge if the format might be adjusted. Be careful: if you demand your own way in some situations it may do you no good at all – you may be better to live with, and make the best of, the planned or routine arrangements. Different situations demand different approaches, and sometimes a specific suggestion will be welcomed.

Broadly the options are:

- •)) To take questions at any time throughout the presentation (this should only be done if you are able and willing to keep control as it can prove disruptive, certainly to time-keeping. Also you must be sure you are going to cope well with the questions or an early one that gets you flustered can dent the best of starts)

- •)) Taking questions at the end of the session (though this can frustrate the audience and may give you a false sense of security if, while you speak uninterrupted, you believe that everything you are saying is being completely accepted)

- •)) A mix of both, perhaps a main question session at the end, but one or two others encouraged or allowed on the way through (these can be prompted at moments when the talk will benefit from some interaction or feedback)

- •)) No questions at any time (though the formal session may be followed by something else that does facilitate questions. Such include an informal chat between members of the audience over some form of refreshments afterwards).

Most presentations may well be followed by questions; indeed you may wish to prompt them to create discussion or debate, or simply to avoid an embarrassing gap at the end of the session. One important point is relevant here. You will often do best to keep the last word of the whole session for yourself. A common danger of a question session is that it tails away at the end and thus, especially if someone else is in the Chair, the final word is taken away from you. What can happen is that, after a few questions, they are slower coming, the last one is somewhat insubstantial perhaps and the Chair ends the meeting: *Well there seem to be no more questions, let's leave it there and thank our speaker ...*

A better route can be to introduce question time in a way that reserves the right to the speaker of the final word. This can be done even through the Chair: *Right, Mr Chairman, perhaps we should see if there are any questions. Then perhaps I could reserve two minutes to summarise before we close.* Few people taking the Chair will take exception to that, still less so if everything is going well.

Directing questions

Sometimes you need to prompt comments and questions, as perhaps at a committee meeting. There are formal inputs, but you also – especially if you are in the Chair – may want to canvass opinion. There are several ways of directing questions. You can use:

- •)) **Overhead questions:** that is questions put to the group generally, and useful for opening up a subject (if there is no response, then you can move on to the next method): *Right, what do you think the key issue here is? Anyone?*

- •)) **Overhead and then directed at an individual:** this method is useful to make the whole group think before looking for an answer from one person: *Right, what do you think the key issues here are? Anyone? ... John, what do you think?*

- •))) **Direct to individual:** this is useful for obtaining individual responses, and testing for understanding: *'John, what do you think ...?'*

- •))) **Non-response/rhetorical questions:** this is useful where you want to make a point to one or more persons in the group without concentrating on anyone in particular, or for raising a question you would expect to be in the group's mind and then answering it yourself: *What's the key issue? Well, perhaps it's ...*

All these methods represent very controlled discussion: dialogue that goes from speaker to group member to speaker and then to another group member (or more), and finally... back to the speaker.

In addition, bear in mind these two types of question, the use of which can help to open up a discussion:

- •))) **Re-directed questions:** useful to prompt discussion and involvement in the group and answer questions posed to you: *That's a good point, John. What do you think the answer is, Mary?* This makes people think and creates involvement, rather than simply providing an answer by the speaker directed at one individual

- •))) **Developmental questioning:** where you take the answer to a previous question and move it around the audience, building on it and asking further questions: *Having established that, how about ...?*

Whichever of the above is being used, and this depends primarily on the relative importance of the topic raised, certain principles should be borne in mind. When you use questions to create involvement, then for what you do to be effective, the following general method may be a useful guide to the kind of sequence that can be employed:

- •))) **State the question clearly and concisely:** questions should relate directly to the subject being discussed. Whenever possible they should require people to think, to draw on their past experiences, and relate them to the present circumstances

-))) **Ask the question first to the group rather than to an individual:** if the question is directed to a single individual, others are off the hook and do not have to think about the answer. Direct, individual questions are more useful to break a general silence in the group, or to involve someone who is not actively participating in the discussion and who you want to draw in

-))) **After asking the question ... pause:** Allow a few moments for the group to consider what the answer should be; do not be tempted to rush on, embarrassed by the silence, and provide an answer in a way that curtails any involvement. Then, if silence continues:

-))) **Ask a specific individual to answer:** and give them a moment to think too. This four-step process starts the entire group thinking because they never know who will be called on. Thus everyone has to consider each question you ask, and be ready to participate. Even those who are not called on are still involved.

To be sure of using an effective questioning technique, there are some things which should be avoided, such as:

-))) **Asking yes or no questions:** participants can attempt to guess the answer (and may be right). These questions should not be used if you want participants to use their reasoning power and actively participate

-))) **Asking unanswerable questions:** you want to provide information, not confusion. Be sure that the knowledge and experience of your group are such that at least some participants can answer any questions you are asking. Never attempt to highlight ignorance by asking questions, which the group cannot handle. And this is particularly true when you are trying to draw out a silent participant and involve them. Be sure they can answer before you ask them the questions. Though incidentally, there is another kind of unanswerable question, posed rhetorically, simply for humorous effect. Such include the likes of: *Why is abbreviated such a long word? Why is a boxing ring square? Why does the partner who snores* *always go to sleep first? What does occasional furniture do the rest of the time?* And many more no doubt, providing another way of injecting a brief light touch

·)) **Asking personal questions:** personal questions are usually rather sensitive, even in one-to-one sessions. They are often inappropriate in a group session. Though again there can be exceptions, which then make an impact. I sometimes ask a group member, *Are you married?* And always get a sort of double take – it is just not the sort of question expected in a business presentation. This is in the context of talking about avoiding bland language, *If I said your wife/husband was 'quite nice', you are entitled to be upset, they are surely far more than that …*

·)) **Asking leading questions:** by leading questions, I mean ones in which the speaker indicates the preferred answer in advance: *Mary, don't you agree that this new form will help solve the problem?* Such questions require little effort on the part of the participant, and will often just annoy. In addition, even if Mary did not agree, she would probably be uncomfortable saying so, given that rejection is apparently not being invited. It is especially important not to lead in this way if you are the most senior person present in an organisational setting

·)) **Repeating questions:** do not make a practice of repeating the question for an inattentive person. Doing so simply encourages further inattention and wastes valuable time. Instead, ask someone else to respond. People will quickly learn that they have to listen. This is especially useful in something like a committee situation – did you ever attend a committee meeting that finished early?

·)) **Allowing group answers:** unless written down (and then referred to around the group), questions that allow several members of the group to answer are not particularly useful. First, everyone cannot talk at once. Second, with group answers a few participants may well tend to dominate the session. And third, group answers allow the silent person to hide and not participate as they should.

The two invaluable and unbreakable rules all sessions should have regarding participation and involvement, both being clearly understood and adhered to, are:

- •)) Only one person can talk at a time

- •)) Whoever is in the Chair decides who that is.

Above all, in this area let your questioning be natural. Ask because you want to know – because you want this information to be shared with the group. Never think of yourself as a quizmaster with certain questions that must be asked whether or not they are timely. Let your manner convey your interest in the response you are going to get, and be sure that your interest is genuine. Forced, artificial enthusiasm will never fool a group.

In many situations none of these things may be necessary; all you have to do is answer questions that are put to you. So, let us think about how that can be done effectively.

Handling questions

When questions do come, prompted, expected or otherwise, you need to think about how you answer them. The following suggested approach will help:

- •)) Get the question right and never try to answer a point when you are actually not quite clear what is meant. If necessary ask for it to be repeated, check it back, *What you are asking is ... is that correct?* Make a quick written note of it if this helps

- •)) If the question was clear to you, but might not have been heard at the back of the room, that is behind the questioner, then either check this first or simply go straight to repeating it, saying it is for the benefit of others. Then, with the question clear, you can proceed to:

- •)) Acknowledge the question and questioner: *Okay, Sue's asking for a comment about …* Not least everything so far gives you a few moments to think, something that is often useful

- •)) Give short informative answers whenever possible, and link to other parts of your message, as appropriate. If necessary it does no harm to say something like, *Right. Let me think about that for a moment.* You cannot then pause for long, but even an additional few seconds may help you get an answer straight in your mind; an audience expecting a considered response will not see this as unacceptable, maybe the reverse.

If you opt, which you may want to, for questions at any time, then remember that to keep things flowing it is perfectly acceptable to:

- •)) Hold them for a moment until you finish making a point, *Good point, let me come to it in just a minute*

- •)) Delay them; saying you will come back to it, in context, when you get to a specific topic area. Then you must remember. Make a note of both the point and who made it

- •)) Refuse them. Some may be irrelevant or likely to lead to too much of a digression, but be *careful* not to do this too often, to respect the questioner's feelings, and to explain why you are doing so (maybe something is better handled later in another meeting, for instance)

- •)) Say: *I don't know.* If you don't know the answer, you *must* say so. You can offer to find out, you can see if anyone else in the group knows, you can make a note of it for later, but if you attempt, unsuccessfully, to answer you will lose all credibility. No-one, in fact, expects you to be omniscient, so do not worry about it: if you are well prepared it will not happen often in any case.

A final dimension here is worth additional comment. Some 'questions' (or statements) may be negative, contradictory – or both.

Handling objections

If your presentations are not contentious and are strictly one way, then objections may well be no problem. If, however, you actually do get objections voiced then they must be dealt with carefully. The first rule is to make sure you have the point made straight in your mind before you respond (remember the maxim, quoted earlier, that it is best to engage the brain before the mouth). There is nothing to say you cannot respond to a question with another question to clarify the query. Or repeat it back, varying the words: *What you are asking is ... Have I got that right?* Similarly, you may want to delay an answer, and there is no reason why doing so cannot be made to sound perfectly acceptable: *That's certainly something I have to explain, perhaps I can pick it up, in context, when I get to ...* Objections can be delayed just as can any other kind of question.

It is wise also not to rush into an answer to an objection. Give it a moment (and yourself time to think – you may be amazed, and relieved, how much can go on in your mind even in a pause of just two or three seconds, a gap that is not a problem to the audience who may, in any case, expect you to consider the matter). Remember also that too glib an answer may be mistrusted, especially one that rushes straight in and starts, *Ah, but ...* A slight pause giving the impression of consideration may be just what is needed here. A pause and an acknowledgement go well together, and also extend your private thinking time. It works well especially if the acknowledgement can be positive and make it clear you are not denying the point – or at least the relevance of it. Phrases like, *That's a good point* really can be appropriate; better still, something that makes it clear that you are going to respond or explain further: *You're right. Cost is certainly a key issue. It is a great deal of money, let me say a word more about why I believe it is a good investment ...* Remember the answer may need to make a point to the whole audience rather than only to the individual who voiced doubts.

A final – important – point here. As has been said, never be afraid to say, *I don't know*. You can offer to check a point later, you can ask if others in the group know, but the dangers of bluffing are all too apparent. You can end up having dug a very deep hole for yourself. However, do consider – in advance – what may come up. A good many questions, and objections too for that matter, are surely wholly expected. You know, if you think about it, the kind of thing that is likely to be raised in a particular situation. Certainly it is no good identifying something as a possible problem and then doing nothing except hope that it will not materialise. You need to have answers in mind for matters that are likely to need dealing with; though realistically you must tailor them to particular circumstances.

Audiences are not, of course, entirely homogeneous groups. All sorts of people may be present (this affects the intentions of the speaker, as has already been intimated) but it also affects the handling of questions. Different people have different attitudes, motivations and manners and may put questions in many different ways. The following section sets out some examples of types of questioner and something of the tactics suitable to deal with each. Some are all too common, others you will rarely have to deal with, and still others only occur when question sessions slip into more open discussion.

Dealing with different styles of questioner

The 'show-off'

- ·)) Avoid embarrassing or shutting them off; you may need them later.

- ·)) Solution: toss them a difficult question. Or say, *That's an interesting point. Let's see what the group thinks of it.*

The 'quick reactor'

•)) Can also be valuable later, but can keep others out of the discussion.

•)) Solution: thank them; suggest we put others to work.

The 'heckler'

•)) This one argues about every point being made.

•)) Solution: Remain calm. Agree, affirm any good points, but toss bad points to the group for discussion. They will be quickly rejected. Privately try to find out what it is that is bothering such a person, try to elicit their co-operation.

The 'rambler'

•)) Who talks about everything except the subject under discussion.

•)) Solution: At a pause in their monologue, thank them, return to and restate relevant points of discussion and go on.

The 'mutual enemies'

•)) When there is a clash of personalities between members of the audience.

•)) Solution: Emphasise points of agreement, in a way that minimises differences. Or frankly ask that personalities be left out of things. Draw attention back to the point being made.

The 'pig-headed'

•)) A person who absolutely refuses, perhaps through prejudice, to accept points that are being discussed.

•)) Solution: Throw their points to the group, have them straighten the person out. Mention that time is short, that you will be glad to discuss it with them later.

The 'digresser'

- •)) Who takes the discussion too far off track.

- •)) Solution: Take the blame yourself. Say, *Something I said must have led you off the subject; this is what we should be discussing ...*

The 'professional gripe'

- •)) Who makes frankly political points.

- •)) Solution: Politely point out that we cannot change policy here; the objective is to operate as best we can under the present system. Or better still, have a member of the group answer him.

The 'whisperers'

- •)) Who hold private conversations which, while they could be related to the subject, are distracting.

- •)) Solution: Do not embarrass them. Direct some point to one of them by name, ask an easy question. Or repeat the last point and ask for comments. Get them away from their separate conversation.

The 'inarticulate'

- •)) Who has the ideas, but cannot put them across.

- •)) Solution: Say, *Let me repeat that ...* (then put it in clearer language).

The 'mistaken'

- •)) Who is clearly wrong.

- •)) Solution: Say, *That's one way of looking at it, but how can we reconcile that with ...* (state the correct point)?

The 'silent'

•)) Who could be shy, bored, indifferent, insecure, or who just might be taking things in and be listening carefully.

•)) Solution: Depends on what is causing the silence. If the person is bored or indifferent, try asking a provocative question, one you think they might be interested in. If shy, compliment them when they do say something, and then ask them direct questions from time to time to draw them in.

In the Chair

This takes us outside the brief for this book a little; however, it is useful in the context of question sessions to refer to it briefly, indeed some of what has been said in the last few pages is of most relevance if you are in the Chair. So, the checklist that follows, adapted from my book *The Meetings Pocketbook* (Management Pocketbooks), reviews the whole question of chairmanship in any type of business or committee meeting where such a role is necessary.

Checklist

Chairing/leading a meeting: guidelines for conducting the whole meeting (which might include presentation, discussion and debate, and questions).

The person directing the meeting must:

•)) command the respect of those attending

•)) do their homework and come prepared, having read any relevant documents and taken any other action necessary to help them 'take charge' (they should also encourage others to prepare, this makes for more considered and succinct contributions to the meeting and saves time)

•)) be punctual

- •)) start on time (it is also good practice to state an estimated finishing time; people like to know how much time they are setting aside)

- •)) ensure administrative matters will be taken care of correctly (such as refreshments, taking minutes, etc.)

- •)) start on the right note and lead into the agenda

- •)) introduce participants, if necessary (and certainly know who is who themselves – name cards can help at some kinds of meeting)

- •)) set the rules

- •)) control the discussion, and the individual types present (the talkative, the quiet, the argumentative, and more)

- •)) encourage contributions where necessary

- •)) ask questions to clarify (this can be a great time saver)

- •)) always query something unclear at once. (If the meeting runs on when something has been misinterpreted it will take longer to sort out and you will have to recap and re-cover a section)

- •)) ensure everybody has their say

- •)) keep the discussion to the point

- •)) listen, as in **listen**. The leader should resolve any 'But you said ... arguments'

- •)) watch the clock, and remind people of the time pressure

- •)) summarise, clearly and succinctly, where necessary, which usually means frequently

- •)) ensure any necessary decisions are actually made, agreed and recorded

- •)) cope with any upsets, outbursts and emotion

•)) provide the final word (summary) and bring matters to a
conclusion (and link to any final administrative detail:
things like setting another meeting date are often
forgotten)

•)) see, afterwards, to any follow-up action (another great
time waster is people arriving at meetings not having
taken action promised at a previous session)

•)) do all this with patience, goodwill, humour and respect
for the various individuals present.

Being an effective chairperson is a skill that may warrant study and
practice. A good chairperson is likely to be effective as a speaker too;
certainly the two skills go together. For many people being able to
take the Chair, and execute the role effectively, puts you in a useful
position, and the effort needed to ensure you can do so is worthwhile.

One last point to end this chapter – the way a presentation is run and
how the group is handled will have a considerable influence on how
a question session goes. If the presentation is lacklustre, the
audience's attention is not held, or indeed if the content – perhaps a
contentious policy matter – has affected their mood, then any speaker
will tend to get a hard time as questions may be asked frankly to make
a point and catch the speaker out (and perhaps impress others). On
the other hand, a speaker in control of the situation, of apparent
expertise and authority, is always treated with a little more
circumspection when it comes to question time. So, prevention and
cure is a good way of looking at this area. Failing all else, remember
what Professor Roland Smith once said at a company AGM, *I'll
answer some of your questions, the more difficult ones will be answered
by my colleagues.*

Do your homework, know your stuff, do not be afraid to say, I don't
know (although not too often!) and you will handle all the aspects of
audience involvement and questions successfully. Won't you?

CHAPTER 8

Afterword

Desperately accustomed as I am to public speaking
Noël Coward

Takes a sip of water, clears throat and stands up ...

'Ladies and Gentlemen – readers (and to qualify for that description you have to have read your way through to this point, not flicked a page or two in from the back of the book) – at the end of this review of the process of presentation let me conclude by putting one or two matters in context, and looking to the future.

There are essentially two aspects to what must be done to create, maintain and enhance your speaking skills. The first, assisted I hope by reading this book, is to have a sound appreciation of the techniques and processes that make a presentation go well. Knowledge of what works well provides the foundation from which you can work and expand your capabilities. Secondly, you need practice. This can come from attending a course, and – if that involves using video (recording what participants do) – not only having a chance to see how you come over, but to discuss the detail of this with other members of the group and with the tutor. A course will also allow you quickly to see other examples of the kinds of things that have to be tackled in a variety of different presentational situations. Or, of course, you can gain experience from actually making real presentations, and the idea of actively seeking out opportunities to accelerate that experience was mentioned in the text.

Presentation is a skill where the process of adding usefully to your experience is, you will find, never ending. There are a number of ways in which you can continue to acquire knowledge about the techniques:

- ·))) Reading additional books and other references on the topic

- ·))) Seeing training films on the subject

- ·))) Meeting and discussing with colleagues (especially to plan or review actual future talks or run constructive post-mortems on past ones)

- ·))) Rehearsing in front of, and with, colleagues and noting comments before going on to a final version (supervising rehearsals is something I am regularly asked to do as a consultant – an objective view is sometimes necessary if people are getting too close to what will be done, so pick a colleague with no reason to flatter you)

- ·))) Reviewing what you do and aiming to learn from experience: for instance noting things to not do, work on or use again (see the checklist in Chapter 9).

All this means there is certainly opportunity to extend learning and practice, and, make no mistake, whatever you may have done already, presentational skill cannot have too much practice, providing, that is, you remain objective and are prepared to analyse honestly what you do (and take on board any feedback from others). Then you can ensure your techniques will improve continually. Within an organisation it may help to improve skills if people are:

- ·))) Encouraged to rehearse what they have to do

- ·))) Encouraged also to seek out additional opportunities to increase practice opportunities (some companies run internal talks, make certain internal meetings more formal than might otherwise be necessary, and take other similar actions to provide such occasions).

Depending on your position this may be a process with which you can play a part, encouraging members of your staff if you are a manager, for instance. On a personal scale even if you are just on one committee, say, but know that your role may well involve more formal speaking situations, then it is worthwhile to look for ways to extend the practice you get ahead of reaching the more important occasions.

The rewards in corporate and career terms, and in a social context too, of developing good presentational skills are considerable. What is more, good habits do set in, a process that is more likely if you set out to make it so. If you develop the habit of preparing, for example, and develop good habits regarding exactly how you go about it, then you will find your whole approach will act to help the end result. A good system for preparing your notes will prompt you to ask yourself if there should be a visual aid at certain points, and whether there are sufficient of them overall, and to do this more certainly and effectively. Good and sufficient visual aids will, in turn, augment the presentation. The thinking and the process create a positive loop. Moreover, practice will soon begin to take some of the chore out of the whole process. Preparation does not take so long for those who know how to go about it and who have a good system for doing it, for example. Even seemingly awkward factors, such as judging how long a message will take to run through, become more certain with practice.

Beyond all this, to a degree, the sky is the limit. The best presenters make it look very easy, though this may simply disguise careful preparation, rehearsal and execution. Training, study and simply practice and sensible consideration of how you have done can help everyone move towards an acceptable standard. But it can do more than this. Charisma, often regarded (indeed defined) as a gift, actually consists (certainly in part) of intentionally applied techniques. Good eye contact, appropriate verbal emphasis, a careful choice of words and gestures, the confidence to hold a pause – and more – all cumulatively add to the charisma rating someone may be regarded as projecting. But such techniques can all be learned, developed and deployed to enhance the overall effect. This is not to say that such a process is contrived. Something like a genuine enthusiasm is infectious. For the rest, in many ways it adds up to a respect for the audience and the occasion. The last thing people want is to sit through a lacklustre presentation. Those who work at how they do it, use the available techniques appropriately and let their personality contribute, make the best job of it, helping both the audience and themselves. The alternative, a dreary presentation and an audience who resent it, is not a happy one.

Thank you for reading this far. I hope you will find that the content of this book will act as a catalyst, giving you some ideas both to implement and deploy immediately and others to work on and adapt. The rest is up to you. You are the only coach who is always there when you get up to speak. If you have already had some practice, considering what you are doing against the knowledge of the principles set out here will help you seek to achieve an even higher standard. If you are nervously awaiting your first outing: go for it. You now know something of the techniques involved and how they can assist will give you confidence. Aim to surprise yourself: and your audience. You may just find that is fun.'

Sits down. Sighs with relief. Imagines filing the notes under 'Never again', and contemplates a large drink.

> *When audiences come to see us authors*
> *lecture, it is largely in the hope that*
> *we'll be funnier to look at than to read*

Sinclair Lewis

CHAPTER 9

How are you Doing?

You can prompt a great deal of change and improvement when it is necessary simply by analysing what you do. The checklist that follows is arranged under four main areas:

- •)) Content

- •)) Structure

- •)) Manner

- •)) Maintenance of interest.

If things go well under all these headings then there is every chance something will appeal to the audience. You can mark yourself for all those factors listed and resolve if necessary to work at any areas you consider need change.

Presentation performance checklist

Content: what you said

- •)) Clear and understandable

- •)) Level of detail

- •)) Level of technicality

- •)) Logical sequence

- •)) Evidence or proof

- •)) Link to visual aids/documentation

- •)) Relevance to the audience.

Structure: arrangement of content

- •)) Clear objectives

- •)) Overall direction

- •)) Use of signposting

- •)) The Beginning: an effective start/statement of intent

- •)) The Middle: a logical progression

- •)) The End: summary/loose ends/request for action/high note

- •)) Continuity

- •)) Timing.

Manner: impression made

- •)) Personal appearance

- •)) Stance

- •)) Use of gestures

- •)) Projection

- •)) Rapport

- •)) Empathy

- •)) Pace

- •)) Eye contact

- •)) Voice: variety and emphasis

- •)) Management of the speaking environment

- •)) Coping with the unexpected

- •)) Sensitivity.

Maintenance of interest: appeal to audience

- •)) Focus on audience

- •)) Enthusiasm

- •)) Use of examples

- •)) Illustration

- •)) Humour

- •)) Aids: appropriate method/clear images/match what was said/illustrative

- •)) Management of any necessary audience involvement

- •)) Adding 'flourish'

- •)) Overall animation.

You can mark yourself in various ways: a good way is to use four levels of comment. These can be A, B, C and D if you like, or you can give them descriptions such as: Satisfactory/Above average/Below average/Unsatisfactory. By using an even number of ratings you cannot mark yourself 'average': you will then find that the top two ratings may indicate all is well for the moment, but the lower two show that some sort of action or change needs to take place. In this way it is easier to fine-tune what you do and make sure that you gradually get better and better as you discover how things work and what impression you are making with your audiences.

If you get into the habit of coming away from everything you do and spending a moment in analysis you will find this pays dividends in the long term.

Index